Compliments of the Chef

100 Great Recipes from the Innovative Restaurants & Cafes of Berkeley, California

By the Sisterhood of Congregation Beth El with Paul T. Johnston
Illustrated by Ruth Dorman

ARIS BOOKS
Berkeley, California

Library of Congress Cataloging in Publication Data

Johnston, Paul, 1950-
Compliments of the chef.

Includes index.
1. Cookery, International.   I.   Temple Beth El
(Berkeley, Calif.). Sisterhood.   II.   Title.
TX725.A1J58 1985   641.5'09   84-24378
ISBN 0-943186-20-X

Aris Books are published by
Harris Publishing Company, Inc.
1621 Fifth Street
Berkeley, CA 94710

Book trade distribution by Simon and Schuster,
a division of Simon & Schuster, Inc.
Simon & Schuster Building
Rockefeller Center
1230 Avenue of the Americas
New York, NY 10020

Book design by Jeanne Jambu and Kajun Graphics
Cover photograph by Marshall Berman
Edited by Carolyn Miller
Set in Berkeley Oldstyle by Artype, Hercules, California
Printed and bound in the United States

First printing, June 1985
10 9 8 7 6 5 4 3 2

FOREWORD

*I*f cooking and eating are important to you, then this book is a vital guide to our new culinary direction. The same energy and vitality that was spent during the rebellious sixties on campuses all over the country, and especially on the University of California campus in Berkeley, is now being spent in many Berkeley area restaurants producing wonderful food. The philosophy of this new cooking idiom is one of rebellion against the vast anonymous world in which we live, with its processed foods touched only by machine, its crops harvested by machine, its loss of quality, and most of all, its loss of individual significance.

The new cooks have restored a sense of personal importance to the culinary scene by being completely in charge of food preparation. The typical Berkeley restaurant is small, which allows better control. The old culinary rules and traditions have been put aside, and the chef searches for the purest and best ingredients to combine in innovative ways. The result of all this is a new group of sparkling restaurants that are, in no insignificant way, influencing American eating and dining habits.

Here then is a collection of excellent recipes offered by the chefs of many of Berkeley's finest restaurants. Chef Paul T. Johnston's introduction is intelligent and interesting, and he has done an admirable job of scaling down the recipes so they can be easily reproduced at home. And bravo! to the Sisterhood of Congregation Beth El—you've proven once again that dedication and service can produce work of great value.

Marion Cunningham
author, The Fannie Farmer
Baking Book

ACKNOWLEDGMENTS

Sisterhoods and cookbooks seem to go together like. . .Berkeley and great restaurants. It was a combination we couldn't resist. In this, our Sisterhood's second cookbook, we have compiled over one hundred exceptional recipes from many of Berkeley's distinctive restaurants, bakeries, and cafes.

We are indebted to the owners and chefs of these establishments, who graciously responded to our requests and parted with their cherished recipes.

I don't think any of us in the Sisterhood anticipated the amount of work that would ensue when one of our members, Matilde Hollander, rekindled our interest in producing a cookbook. Each Sisterhood member involved has generously and enthusiastically given hours and hours of time to this project. Our sincere thanks go to Donna Weinberg, Ruth Dorman, and Roz Plishner, who not only solicited recipes but also shopped for and participated in the lengthy recipe-testing process in Aris's test kitchen.

The considerable talents of our illustrator, Ruth Dorman, are showcased throughout this book, and her contributions to every aspect of its production cannot be overstated. Lois Schwartz undertook the enormous task of word processing and editing the manuscript and was also an invaluable contributor to the restaurant write-ups. We also benefited from the legal counsel of Judy Koster and from the writing and editing skills of many others.

This project was a true blending of volunteerism and professionalism. It would not have been possible for us to produce this book without Chef Paul T. Johnston. Paul's expertise and knowledge raised the entire book to a professional level that no volunteer group could hope to achieve alone.

And finally, our sincere thanks to Aris Books. We are especially indebted to John Harris and Mimi Luebbermann for gently guiding us, with patience and good humor, through the ins and outs of professional publishing.

Lois Marcus, President
Sisterhood of Congregation Beth El
Berkeley, California

TABLE OF CONTENTS

RESTAURANTS

RECIPE INDEX

Chicken Curry   145
Chicken Paillards with Ancho Chili Butter   142
Chicken with Sweet Basil   145
Duck Sausage Wrapped In Grape Leaves with Zinfandel Sauce   41
Green Chicken Stew with Lemon Grass, Jalapeños, and Lime   69
Petti di Pollo Ripiene (Stuffed Chicken Breasts)   138
Pollo Colorado (Chicken in Red Sauce)   125
Roast Poussins with Green Plum Chutney   98
Suprême de Volaille en Feuilletée (Chicken Breast in Puff Pastry)   34
Suprême de Volaille Parmesan (Boneless Chicken Breasts with Parmesan Cheese)   120

DESSERTS AND PASTRIES
Almond Cake with Raspberry Purée   110
Almond Semifreddo   61
Brie Cheesecake   56
Cheese Puffs   79
Chocolate Bourbon Pecan Pie   85
Chocolate Velvet Pie   79
Lemon Curd Sauce for Fresh Fruit   109
Macadamia Nut and Coconut Tart   63
Pear Tart   50
Pecan Pie   80
Pie Dough   80
Pots de Crème au Chocolat Grand Marnier (Chocolate Custard Cream)   34
Queen of California   73
Rhubarb Pie   149
Sticky Buns   47

EGGS
Huevos Rancheros (Ranch-Style Eggs)   43
Souffléed Apple Pancake   44

FISH
Cold Poached Coho Salmon with Orange Mayonnaise and Watercress Salad   70
Cold Poached Salmon with Cucumber–Sour Cream Sauce   147
Fish with Wild Mushroom–Cream Sauce   121
Petrale Sole Boisliveau (Fillet of Sole Stuffed with Spinach and Endive)   100
Poached Fish with Piccata Sauce   133

A CHEF'S INTRODUCTION TO
BERKELEY'S CULINARY REVOLUTION

*T*his book comes directly from the professional kitchens of Berkeley, through the diligence of the volunteers of the Sisterhood of Congregation Beth El. As a chef and former (and probably future) restaurant owner, I speak the restaurant language and am the translator for this book, formulating recipes for the home kitchen using material from the very different environment of the restaurant kitchen. The greatest challenge has been to do this in all consciousness of, and with all respect for, the spirit of the recipe and the dish it represents. My goal, and that of Aris Books, has been to give you a recipe that, when followed precisely, will give an honest approximation of the actual dish, for a recipe can never be exact.

And it has been an amusing task as well, knowing the time constraints that force a chef to scribble a recipe on the back of his shopping list while the volunteer from the Sisterhood waits, lucky that even though he had forgotten the appointment, she has managed to catch him and he has the presence of mind to jot the recipe down. So we often got shorthand versions of recipes, often had to go back to the chef with questions, and often had to rely on my intuition.

It has been an education to approach the work of my colleagues in this way. I am more accustomed to eating their work, being inspired by it, or talking about it than I am to trying to replicate it in a domestic kitchen. I have learned some new techniques, particularly in the fields of Chinese and Southeast Asian cooking and, not being a baker by predilection, have picked up a few things about bread and desserts that are sure to come in handy some day.

It is important, in trying to understand these recipes, to take their original environment into consideration. The resources, equipment, and manpower available to a chef in his own restaurant are quite unlike anything to be found at home. The chef has a staff that can provide everything from peeled garlic and onions to basic stocks and sauces, as well as such specialized ingredients as any amount of a certain vegetable cut to specific dimensions. A chef has many functions, which vary with the restaurant, and may include planning menus and developing new recipes; food cost and buying (including trips to markets); hiring, firing, and training cooks, and sometimes dishwashers; and actual food production during and before service. And often, the chef owns the restaurant!

With so much responsibility, a chef needs as many resources as possible, the most important of which is input from coworkers. When a kitchen is really alive, the ideas come from everyone, and no chef can claim complete authorship of a recipe. Somewhere, in the background at least, is the suggestion of some other cook, or maybe even the dishwasher, who pointed out that a certain dish was coming back from the table only half eaten.

Where Do Recipes Come From?

Where does a recipe come from, and how does it work in the restaurant? Let's take a look at the kitchen first. A restaurant kitchen, depending on the size of the establishment, usually breaks down into three stations: pasta and sauté, grill or broiler, and salad (also called pantry). If the restaurant is large or the culinary emphasis is away from the grill, pasta and sauté become two separate stations. If the restaurant is small, the grill and sauté stations may merge, and the pantry and pasta may be handled by the same person. But as an example, let's take a grill-oriented restaurant of about seventy-five seats, requiring the three basic stations, sauté, grill, and pantry. A waiter hands in an order for a table of four. It reads:

> Table: 7   No. of guests: 4   Waiter: Joe
> 1 Caesar Salad
> 2 Timbales
> 1 Tomato Basil Fettuccine
> 1 Salmon (Grilled)
> 1 Chicken Paillard
> 1 Salmon (Sautéed)
> 1 Chicken Goat Cheese Linguine

In this kitchen, the pasta and sauté station is first in line, so it gets the orders and coordinates timing (also called expediting). The cook looks at the ticket and sees that the appetizers are all cold and all come from the salad station. She relays the order to the pantry. The pantry cook unmolds and dresses the timbales, which will not suffer while he makes the Caesar salad. He breaks coddled eggs into the bowl he keeps for the Caesars, whisks in the dressing to emulsify, tosses in a handful of prepared romaine lettuce, sprinkles in anchovies, grated Parmesan cheese, and croutons, tosses the salad with his hands, arranges it on the plate, and sets it on the counter. "Up on seven," he calls to the sauté cook. She rings the waiter. He arrives immediately, knowing that a Caesar salad wilts within minutes, and serves his table their first course.

A few minutes later, the waiter says "Fire pasta on seven, please." The sauté cook ignites a burner and in a sauté pan pours olive oil from a wine bottle. In go pine nuts to toast for a minute, then a spoonful of garlic purée for a second, then a splash of white wine and a handful of roasted tomatoes with the flame left high. She flicks up the burner control for the pasta water, which, kept at a simmer already, is engulfed by flame and instantly comes to a rolling boil. She throws in a handful of fresh pasta, gives the sauté pan with the sauce a shake, and adds salt and a pinch of fresh-ground pepper. The sauce is reduced to her satisfaction and she removes it from the fire, adds fresh-chopped basil, tastes the sauce, lifts the basket out of the pasta pan, shakes the noodles dry, adds them to the sauce, tosses the whole works in the air a couple of times to mix it, and slides it on the plate. One hand sprinkles grated Parmesan cheese over the pasta, while the other adds a strewing of chopped parsley. The plate goes up on the counter, and the sauté cook rings the waiter.

As the waiter picks up the pasta, the sauté cook turns to the grill cook and says "Fire four," because she knows that by the time the kitchen has finished cooking the entrées, those four people will have finished their pasta. Nonetheless, the waiter shows up a minute later and repeats the "fire" order. This kind of double-checking has saved his life many times and the kitchen always appreciates it. (Bear in mind that a seventy-five-seat dining room has fifteen to twenty-five tables and the kitchen can be looking at as many as fifteen to twenty tickets at once.) The sauté cook has already prepared the sauce for the pasta (she did it at the same time as the tomato-basil pasta), and she now flours the piece of salmon and starts it cooking in a small sauté pan. The grill cook puts his piece of salmon on and, after waiting a minute, puts the chicken paillard on the grill, having given the thick salmon fillet a head start. He glances at the sauté station to gauge his coworker's progress on table No. 7 (as well as several other tables in progress). He pulls out two plates and arranges the garnishes, turns to two other tables that were just fired, and flips the salmon and the paillard.

Meanwhile, the sauté cook throws another order of pasta in the water, removes the salmon to a warm plate, and splashes brandy into the sauté pan. Flames billow, then die,

and she adds a spoonful of cream sauce base complete with mushrooms, pours in a splash of cream, stirs rapidly with a whisk, adds a shake of salt and a few drops of lemon juice from a wine bottle, tastes, and pours the sauce over the salmon. The grill cook lifts the salmon and chicken from the grill together, puts them on their plates, spoons a dollop of basil butter on the salmon and one of ancho chili butter on the chicken, then slides over and finishes the salmon plate for the sauté cook while she drains the pasta and tosses it with the sauce. It has thickened a bit, so she adds a splash of chicken stock, heats the whole for a second, slides it on the plate, arranges a fan of red pepper julienne over the top, inserts a sprig of mint as garnish, and rings the waiter.

Scenes like this occur every night in hundreds of permutations all over Berkeley, indeed, all over the world. This is the world of the professional cook, where preparedness for the rush is of paramount importance and as few words as possible are spoken between workers to accomplish the end of artfully feeding as many people as the restaurant will hold.

With this sample of restaurant life in mind, it is easy to see the difficulty of formulating a recipe at all, much less one that works dependably at home. Most restaurant recipes are never written down, but are transmitted orally and by demonstration, or are reinvented at every execution, changing to accommodate ingredients and moods.

Where Do Chefs Come From?

In addition to the physical setting there is a host of other influences affecting the cuisine from which these recipes arise. The Bay Area is a vast melting pot of peoples, their cooking, and their ingredients, and this affects anyone who cooks here. Berkeley and its environs have been the site of a unique confluence of politics with education in fields such as nutrition and literature, which, combined with a stagnation of the economy, left college-educated people with more job opportunities in food service than in their chosen field.

A hypothetical, though not necessarily typical example of the making of a chef might be that of a brand-new Ph.D. in history with no money and no job. Unable to leave town, our disgruntled graduate gets a job prepping in a restaurant, and soon realizes that in addition to his European travel experience, his intelligence, and his basic arts training he has a special and exciting sensitivity to food. The restaurant not being one of the best, and the habit of political rebellion still strong, we have here a culinary revolutionary, a person who remembers amazing meals in France, Spain, Italy, and Mexico and sets out to reinterpret them. Skills learned in a professional but uninspired restaurant setting soon lend ability to the tremendous drive of an open mind and exploring curiosity.

There are many versions of this story, many men and women who found that what they thought was their career training was really just a way of getting ready to cook, and—with the Chez Panisse group foremost and earliest—these chefs have taken the variety of cuisines and ingredients in the Bay Area and, with openness, honesty, and imagination, have woven a style no longer in revolt against older cooking modes but a logical extension of them, a cuisine with classical underpinnings and a wholly American character.

What Is California Cuisine?

Although the cuisine that has emerged is hard to define (some practitioners even objecting to the inescapable, but misleading appellation of "California cuisine"), it does have some clear outlines. This style of cooking relies heavily on ingredients of the highest quality and freshness. The emphasis is on simplicity, with extensive use of the mesquite grill and a general direction strongly away from the heaviness associated with French haute cuisine, although many French techniques are of central importance. Sauces are thickened with purées of fruit or vegetables; or by reductions of rich stocks; or by butter worked into, and emulsified by, a strongly acid reduction of citrus juices, wine, vinegar, or fruit juices, or a mixture of these elements. (The basic sauce of this family is called *beurre blanc* and is drawn directly from French cuisine. It is discussed at length in the Basics section). Other characteristics include vegetables cooked *al dente* at most, an emphasis on seafood and away from beef (perhaps in revolt against the steakhouse cooking we all grew up on), and a "smaller is better" attitude resulting in an affection for baby vegetables and lettuces, as well as very young chickens and lamb. In fact, there is a near-fetish regarding ingredients in the Berkeley area, with sources zealously sought and jealously protected and prices inexorably reflecting demand.

One of the most distinctive features of the recent culinary revolution in and around Berkeley is a bold amalgamation of cuisines, with exotic ingredients and techniques made to speak a new language, and elements of non-European cookery finding their way into the most unorthodox settings. Among the influential non-European cuisines in the area are Chinese, Southeast Asian, Mexican and Southwest American, Japanese, and traditional American home and country cookery. While Los Angeles has its Franco-Japanese trend, we have Fourth Street Grill serving two weeks of Indonesian foods; Christopher's Café mixing Chinese, Southeast Asian, French, and California mesquite grill cookery; and frequent appearances of Indian food at Omnivore. Chefs can be found using lemon grass in marinades of their own formulation. Papaya may find its

way into a composed butter or a salad dressing, and other "exotic" elements such as an array of Indian spices, dried Persian limes, dried chilies, Italian dried tomatoes, assorted caviars, and *galangal*, may turn up in heretofore unfamiliar circumstances and combinations. (These and other unusual items are discussed in more detail in the Ingredients section.)

Along with the "new California" restaurants found in this book are other restaurants that are either wholly ethnic or deserve institutional status for having survived decades in the toughest business Dun and Bradstreet ever rated.

The Berkeley food phenomenon is the result of experimentation and unbridled creativity. I, for one, will be satisfied if this book can be used in that spirit, as a road map leading first to regions charted by chefs and other professionals (who, after all, started out as amateurs), and then to regions of your own discovery.

Paul T. Johnston

INGREDIENTS

*I*t is basic to the Berkeley culinary phenomenon that all ingredients are special and that the ingredients dictate the recipe, not the other way around. Many of Berkeley's best dishes are the result of conforming the cooking to the best ingredients available. While the purpose of this section is to describe some of the unusual ingredients used in this book, it should be remembered that one aim of this kind of cooking is not necessarily to use a certain unusual thing, but to use the *best* ingredients, unusual or not.   PTJ

Bamboo Shoots

The presliced bamboo shoots available in supermarkets are tasteless and have poor texture. Canned whole bamboo shoots are a great improvement. Before using them, slice them in half lengthwise and rinse them well under running water and slice to the desired size. *Sources:* Some regular grocery stores may carry whole bamboo shoots, but the best bet is an Asian grocery store. Some Asian markets are now carrying fresh bamboo shoots packed in water.

Butter

Most of the recipes in this book were tested using unsalted butter; when we consider it especially important to a recipe, it is specified.

Salt is used in butter not so much as a flavoring as it is a preservative; saltiness often covers up a certain amount of rancidity. The objection to salted butter is not to the salt but to the possible lack of freshness. Sweet butter can be tricky to buy. Get it from a store with a high turnover. If you are not going to use it within a few days, freeze most of it, as it will go rancid. If you have doubts about the butter you are going to buy, unwrap a corner and smell it. If there is the slightest hint of sourness, go elsewhere. *Sources:* Most supermarkets and grocery stores.

Chicken Breasts

Boneless chicken breasts are used extensively in this book. You can either bone them yourself or have the butcher do it. (An old-fashioned poultry shop is ideal for this.) When buying chicken breasts to bone, avoid the halved breasts sold in most grocery stores. They are hard to work with. Also, since they are rarely split in half accurately, there is usually a lot of waste.

Chilies and Peppers

Used in Mexican, Asian, Mediterranean, and California cooking, the chili in its hundreds of varieties is used sometimes as a vegetable, sometimes as a seasoning.

Bell Peppers

The familiar green bell pepper turns red when ripe, becoming sweeter and more complex-tasting in the process. Other varieties turn golden yellow or even black. They are eaten raw in salads, are used roasted and peeled in many different preparations, and are eaten as a vegetable. *Sources:* Widely available in supermarkets and grocery stores.

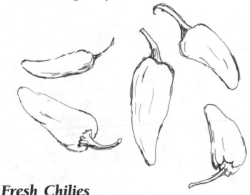

Fresh Chilies

Fresh chilies figure largely in local cooking, as an object of a heat fetish and as the source of unique flavors. The heat of chili in some dishes is not just a physical sensation, but an integral part of the flavor structure. There are hundreds of different chilies. Following are the ones used in this book, listed in order of diminishing heat. Be advised, however, that the heat of fresh chilies varies; one batch of *jalapeños* may be bland, while the supposedly mild Fresno chili can sometimes knock your socks off.

Thai Chili: This is the hottest commercially grown chili we have ever met; it has driven seasoned jalapeño eaters to gasping despair. It is a tiny chili, ¼ inch wide and 2 to 3 inches long, but watch out. Like all peppers, it turns red when ripe.

Jalapeño Chili: This is a widely available chili. It is dark green, often with bluish-black shadings, about an inch wide and 2- to 3-inches long, with a blunt, rounded shape. When cut open, it has a pungent aroma that is an indication of its heat. The stronger the aroma, the hotter the chili. This is the chili to use in most Thai dishes, unless the Thai chili is called for. When ripe, the jalapeño turns red, has a sweeter flavor and is at its absolute hottest.

Serrano Chili: A small chili that packs a mighty wallop. Some consider it hotter than the jalapeño. About 2 inches long and ½ inch wide, it is a lighter green than the jalapeño and some turn yellow and red when ripe. The *serrano* has a taste reminiscent of black pepper and is much used in *salsa crudas*.

Fresno Chili: This is a milder chili, sometimes with only a hint of heat. It is similar in size to a jalapeño but conical in shape and a lighter green. When ripe, they turn beautiful yellows and reds. They are good to use when the flavor of chili is wanted but not the heat.

Pasilla, Poblano, and Anaheim Chilies: These are usually but *not* always mild chilies. The Anaheim is about 6 inches long and 1½ inches wide, and pale green in color. The *poblano* and *pasilla* are both dark green and roughly 3-inch elongated triangles. These chilies turn red when ripe and are dried at that stage, when they are often mildly hot. They have tough skins when fresh and should be peeled. *Sources:* Fresh chilies are found in the greatest variety in produce markets serving

Latin or Asian populations. Some gourmet markets are beginning to carry fresh chilies.

Dried Chilies

Dried chilies are important flavorings in Mexican cooking and are available in vast variety. Although not much used in this book, they do play a significant part in the cooking of some Berkeley chefs. The most widely used dried chilies, outside of Mexican cuisine, are the hottest ones, from cayenne to red pepper flakes. Cayenne is made from a small African red chili. Red pepper flakes are usually made from the Japanese red chili. It is often best to make your own pepper flakes, because the flavor begins to dissipate on grinding, leaving nothing but heat. The other commonly used dried chilies are made from larger ripe chilies such as the *ancho, poblano,* and *pasilla.* They are usually mildly hot, being used for their flavor, not their heat. *Sources:* Dried chilies can be found in Mexican markets.

Clarified Butter

Perhaps the finest of cooking oils, clarified butter is butter with the moisture and milk solids removed. It tolerates very high heat and lends the flavor and body of butter to a dish. It is expensive, about double the price of butter, and it requires a little effort to make. There are several methods for making it. The simplest (but not the best) is to melt butter and then chill it. The butterfat will rise to the top, and the liquid and solids will sink to the bottom. The problem is separating the two components without wasting butter or getting unwanted moisture in the clarified butter. A better, but more time-consuming, method is to gently simmer melted butter. The milk solids will appear at the top as foam, where they can be skimmed off. The moisture will simply evaporate. There are more elaborate methods, for which you might consult an Indian cookbook recipe for ghee.

Coconut Milk

Most restaurants use canned coconut milk, and we have found that the frozen varieties are best. Siam Cuisine specifies a Thai brand. All of these are basically a purée of fresh coconut meat. Sweetened coconut milk is for desserts and piña coladas and does not work for these recipes. You can make your own coconut milk by soaking finely grated fresh or dried coconut in hot water for about an hour, then puréeing the mixture in a blender and straining out the liquid. Generally two or three extractions are made from the same meat, and many recipes specify different uses for each extraction. For these recipes, make two extractions and combine them. Homemade coconut milk will be a different strength than the canned (probably weaker, having a greater water content) so pay close attention to the liquid level of your dish and cook it down if necessary. *Sources*: Thai, Vietnamese, Indian, and Chinese grocery stores; some gourmet markets or delis; the frozen-food case of large grocery stores.

Crème Fraîche

Crème fraîche is simply cultured heavy cream. It is widely used as a substitute for heavy cream and sour cream. Since it is cultured, it has a slightly sour, cheesy taste. Unlike sour cream, it can be boiled without curdling. It can also be whipped and sweetened and used in desserts.

To make *crème fraîche*, add ¼ cup of buttermilk or unflavored yogurt to 2 cups of heavy cream. Mix well and let the mixture stand in a warm place overnight or until the desired sourness is achieved.

Dried Lemon Leaves

A component of Indonesian and Thai cooking, dried lemon leaves are just that and not really so exotic, especially if you have a lemon tree in your backyard. That's your ingredient right there, on the ground. Like lemon grass, lemon leaves have the taste of lemon without the acidity. *Sources*: Southeast Asian grocers or the backyard.

Dried Limes and Lime Leaves

Dried limes are available whole, called "dried Kaffir limes," or in the form of strips of dried peel. They have an intense lime flavor and an aroma made more complex by the drying process, and are used in Thai and Indonesian curries and some Mideastern dishes, as are the dried leaves. The limes are used crushed, the leaves are used whole or crumbled, the dried peel whole. Both the peel and the leaves are often called *makrud* or *macrut*. *Sources*: Asian or Mideastern grocery stores.

Fish Sauce

Fish sauce is one of those foreign seasonings we could call exotic but which a not-so-open-minded person might call weird. It looks like soy sauce, but is lighter in color, and serves the same function, as a source of salt and flavor depth, but it actually consists of the brine from pickled fish. This gives it a distinctive aroma. Fish sauce is an essential ingredient of Southeast Asian cooking; it cannot be omitted without affecting the flavor of a dish. The fishy odor is noticeable only before cooking. The saltiness varies with the brand; you should taste first and adjust the recipe accordingly. In general, fish sauce is twice as salty as soy sauce. *Sources*: Thai, Vietnamese, or Chinese grocers.

Galangal

Related to ginger, *galangal* is a recent discovery to most of us in this country. It looks like ginger, but is woodier and has an aroma like genuine spirits of turpentine (which is not to be confused with paint thinner). Used mainly for seasoning soups and stews, it is hard to find in the fresh state, but is available in powdered form (called *laos* powder) and as dried slices. The dried slices are tough and woody and should be powdered in a blender or food processor, or simmered in the dish and removed before serving. *Sources*: Thai, Vietnamese, or Indian grocers; sometimes found fresh in produce markets.

Garlic

Garlic is nearly a cult food, and a lot of it is eaten in Berkeley. Vital to most cuisines and a source of both powerful and subtle flavors, its importance cannot be overstated. When shopping for garlic, look for large heads with large cloves. Small cloves are hard to peel and dry

out quickly. As with other foods, freshness is important, and if you have never had garlic fresh out of the ground, it is worth the trouble. Fresh garlic is more delicate and fragrant than older garlic, which starts to become acrid after a few months. Look for garlic that is still moist between the cloves, with the dividing parchment soft and pliable rather than crisp and papery. Avoid using cloves that are yellowed and withered. Avoid those little cellophane-wrapped boxes traditionally sold in supermarkets. Look for a produce market where the bulbs are displayed openly in a bin. And if you don't like what is displayed, ask if they have anything fresher in the back. Produce markets buy most of their year's garlic in July and August when the American garlic crop is harvested. Mexican garlic is harvested twice a year, and can be superb. When you do find a good batch, buy a month's worth and store it in a cool, dark place away from moisture. *Sources*: Produce markets, ethnic grocery stores, gourmet markets.

Ginger

A pungent rhizome widely used in Asian cookery. The ginger used in this book is almost always fresh. *Sources:* Fresh ginger is now available in supermarkets across the country.

Herbs

There is not room in this book for an exhaustive discussion of herbs, but we can cover a few principles. Berkeley cooking relies heavily on the use of fresh herbs—the flavors of fresh herbs are truer and more interesting in general than those of their dried counterparts.

Sources: Dried herbs are available from supermarkets, delis, and gourmet markets, as well as the spice sections of many ethnic markets. Some produce markets carry fresh herbs, but the best source is your own garden. Most herbs are easy to grow and forgiving of mistakes. There is incomparable satisfaction in stepping out to your garden or even a few potted plants and snipping off a fresh sprig of this or that. Herbs make attractive borders, and you are assured of a supply of what are often scarce and expensive commodities. This is also a good way to slip into the very European (and very Berkeley) practice of keeping a kitchen garden, which might come to include your own patch of lettuces and baby vegetables.

Basil: Considered by some to be the queen of herbs, basil comes in a bewildering array of varieties in nurseries. The commercially grown sweet basil is the most widely used in cooking, however. There is nothing like fresh basil, especially not dried basil. Except for a pizza-hound tomato sauce or some Creole dishes, there is very little use for dried basil in Berkeley. We tend to go without during the winter, just to make that first plate of *pasta al pesto* taste better.

Bay Leaf: Use only the leaf of the Turkish bay laurel. This shrub grows well in mild climates and is said to do well indoors. Commercial dried bay leaves vary in quality. Look for leaves that still have some color and moisture.

Cilantro: Also known as Chinese parsley, this fragrant herb consists of the leaves of the coriander plant. Considered by some to be an acquired taste (mostly those who have yet to

acquire the taste) cilantro is essential to authentic Mexican, Southeast Asian, Indian, Mideastern, and some Chinese cooking. Its delicate perfume completes the flavor combinations of garlic, ginger, spices, and, especially, chilies. *Sources*: Most produce markets, especially in Latin and Chinese neighborhoods.

Oregano and Marjoram: These cousins are widely confused and have many variants and subspecies and may be subspecies of each other. They look much alike; marjoram has reddish stems and small heart-shaped leaves and a perfumey, soapy fragrance. Oregano has darker stems, larger heart-shaped leaves and a fragrance reminiscent of pencil shavings. Neither fresh herb bears much resemblance to its dried form. Dried oregano is used in Mexican cooking and in Italian dishes. Dried marjoram is also used in Italian cooking, but it usually loses so much in the drying process that it might as well be left out.

Tarragon: This herb with its sweet licorice flavor is a French favorite and is well loved by many, although some people cannot bear it. It has been overused often, especially in its dried form, when it is stronger and less subtle than when fresh. Only French tarragon has the proper strength of flavor. If using dried tarragon, take care not to overdo it.

Thyme: The plant looks like a miniature evergreen shrub. It grows 12 to 18 inches high and has short dark-green needlelike leaves. There are many varieties, including silver, lemon, English, and creeping, and many "standard" types with confusing nomenclature. It is one of the most basic herbs, part of the traditional bouquet garni, and is used in stocks, as a poultry seasoning, and as an essential seasoning in many French dishes. This herb dries very well and quality brands are perfectly acceptable, although fresh thyme does have a nicer flavor.

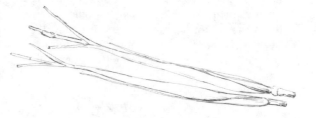

Lemon Grass

Lemon grass looks like a large, coarse scallion and has the flavor and aroma of lemon without the tartness. It is used as a flavoring, like bay leaves, and not eaten by itself. *Sources*: Fresh lemon grass can be impossible to find in some parts of the country. Check in areas with Southeast Asian populations, or try asking at one of their restaurants. It is easy to grow; this is what most restaurants do. It is widely available in the Bay Area, in produce markets and in Chinatown. As a substitute for fresh lemon grass, use dried lemon grass tea, or check in an Indian grocery store for the powdered form, which may be called *"sereh poeder"* and is packaged by a Dutch exporter.

Mushrooms

From the pedestrian but serviceable *Agaricus bisporus* available commercially, to the seasonal boletuses, morels, and chanterelles, mushrooms have lent interest to the table for eons. Mushrooms of all types have recently become popular. It is now possible to buy fresh wild mushrooms in season at produce markets, as well as a wide variety of cultivated types.

Cultivated Mushrooms

In addition to the commercial mushrooms we have all used many times, growers are now producing a variety of Asian mushrooms. *Enoki*, or *straw mushrooms*, are tiny white fungi that grow in clumps and have an utterly charming appearance. They are used in salads and as a garnish and plate decoration, though their flavor contributes little. *Oyster mushrooms* are widespread wild mushrooms and one of the most successfully cultivated varieties. They grow on dead wood and are said to have a faint flavor of seafood. This is more true of the wild than the domestic variety. *Black forest*, or *shiitake*, mushrooms are another Asian type now widely cultivated. The fresh variety has excellent cooking characteristics, and it is refreshing to see a domesticated wild thing with such personality. *Sources*: Produce markets and supermarkets.

Wild Mushrooms

Now we enter the field of the arcane. While identification of most edible mushrooms is a simple matter, mistakes have dread implications. In the Bay Area, seasonal wild mushrooms are available in produce and gourmet markets, who procure them from proven sources.

Chanterelle: *(Cantherellus cibarius)* This beautiful mushroom is apricot yellow and aromatic, and is one of the choicest and easiest to identify of the wild mushrooms. They have a strong affinity for cream and white wine.

Field Mushroom: *(Agaricus campestris)* This mushroom is much like the commercial mushroom (which was bred from it), but has a characteristic "wild" flavor. It is tricky to identify because some of its close relatives cause stomach complaints in some people, and because in the button phase there is a danger of confusing it with a deadly amanita.

Morel: *(Morchella augusticeps, Morchella esculenta)* Considered by many to be the finest of wild mushrooms, the morel is also the easiest to identify, and one of the most expensive.

Cèpe (Boletus edulis): Another very choice mushroom, available most often in the dried form and called *porcini*. It is the object of intense and secretive searching during the fall months after the rains begin. This mushroom is happiest combined with meats, game, red wine.

Dried Mushrooms

Morels, *porcini* (or *cèpes*), and *shiitake* mushrooms are most widely available in dried form. Drying accentuates and transforms mushroom flavors so that the dried product is really a different ingredient from the fresh. The shiitake, or black forest, mushroom is a basic ingredient in some Asian dishes, while the porcini, or cèpe, is used extensively in French and Italian cooking. Dried morels are used in the same way as cèpes, especially with game. *Sources:* Gourmet markets, Italian delis; at very high prices (fortunately, a little goes a long way). Shiitakes are available from Asian grocers and sometimes in the Oriental food sections of supermarkets.

Olive Oil

Talking about olive oil gets to be like talking about wine. The range and subtlety of the topic invite book-length discussion. Dating back to antiquity, olive oil has been a primary source of human nourishment. In its current use, it is still one of the most basic ingredients of Mediterranean cuisine and fits naturally into the "California-Mediterranean" style that characterizes much of Berkeley's best cooking.

It takes at least two kinds of olive oil to stock your kitchen for the recipes in this book. First you should have a solid but not terribly expensive olive oil for basic cooking needs and as the base for many salad dressings and mayonnaises. The other olive oil you will need is one of the extra-virgin grade. This oil will be used mostly as a flavoring. Its delicate aromatic character suffers from cooking, while its strength can be overwhelming. And, of course, intermediate grades and strengths give the cook more flexibility. When buying the expensive olive oils, try a small bottle first. Also, unless they suit your taste, avoid dark or green olive oils; they can be very strong and acrid tasting. The preferred oil is extra-virgin grade, from Italy, France, Greece, Spain, or California. Price is not always the best indication of quality. Experiment—it's fun. *Sources*: Gourmet markets, Italian delicatessens, and even supermarkets carry olive oil. Supermarkets may be the cheapest places to buy quantities of standard-grade olive oil, but may not carry the fancier varieties.

Parmesan Cheese

There is only one kind of genuine Parmesan cheese, Parmigiano Reggiano. This cheese is strictly controlled by Italian law, aged at least eighteen months, and produced only three months of the year in a limited area of the country. It is handmade and necessarily expensive. At its best, when freshly cut from the wheel, it should be moist and grate easily, and should be served within minutes of grating. Store it well wrapped in your refrigerator and go ahead and use it within a couple of weeks. This absolutely extraordinary cheese makes an astounding difference in any dish calling for freshly grated cheese, and is vital to pastas, *risotti*, and a host of other Italian and California dishes. *Sources*: Italian grocers and gourmet markets.

Other Grating Cheeses

In this country "Parmesan cheese" has come to mean any aged, hard grating cheese, and some serviceable cheeses fall into this category. The most important thing to know is that any cheese begins giving up its soul to the atmosphere as soon as it is grated. So never waste your money on pre-grated cheese. Buy the best-quality "Parmesan cheese" you can afford, by the chunk, and grate it yourself. The standard box-type cheese grater does an adequate job if you are grating just enough for a meal. Although not in the league of a Reggiano Parmesan, a good grade of domestic grating cheese will serve your needs until you can splurge on the real thing. In addition to the domestic version of Parmesan, there is a class of Italian cheeses called *grana,* which have more character and cost more than our domestic Parmesans. If you are going to cook the cheese, one of these lesser "Parmesans" will be more than adequate. *Sources*: Italian grocers, delicatessens, gourmet markets.

Sun-dried Tomatoes

This is currently a chic ingredient, and for good reason. The rich flavor of vine-ripened tomatoes acquires overtones of figs or raisins through the drying process. The tomatoes are split open lengthwise, salted, and dried in the sun in Southern Italy, where strings of drying tomatoes festoon the exteriors of many houses. After drying, the tomatoes are packed in olive oil or shipped dry, like dried fruit. Dried tomatoes are used in pastas, pizzas, sandwiches, and many other applications. *Sources*: Italian grocers, delicatessens, gourmet markets.

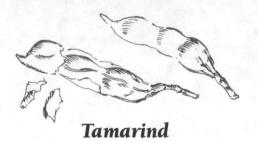

Tamarind

The pulp from the seed pod of a leguminous tree, tamarind is both tart and sweet. It is one of the flavors in cola drinks and is used as the basis of an Italian soda called *tamarindo*. It is also widely used in Mexican and South American cooking. The pulp is dark and gooey, almost gelatinous. To use the creature whole, peel the husk from the pod and extract the seeds from the pulp. Place the extracted pulp in a bowl or jar and cover it with boiling water, then let it soak for at least an hour. Then mash it together with your fingers and force the liquid through a sieve. And, yes, there is an easier way, which I found after several years of this struggle. Indian groceries carry a tamarind extract (Aeroplane brand) which is roughly the same strength as extracted tamarind pulp. And, for once, the processed product is as good as the natural one. *Sources:* Fresh whole tamarind can be found in the more complete produce markets, Asian stores, and Latino markets. The concentrate is available in Indian grocery stores.

Thai Perfumed Rice

This is another unfamiliar product, which after a heroic local search by Ruth Dorman was located in the community of San Pablo, California, in a tiny Vietnamese grocery store. It is a rice that is said to be scented with jasmine flowers. When cooked there is no hint of flowery aroma, but the rice is delicious: rich, fragrant, and nutty, unlike regular supermarket rice. It should be washed well and then cooked like any other white rice. *Sources:* Give yourself plenty of time and use the phone. Several grocers said they could order it for us, but then we would never have found that great little store. Perfumed rice is inexpensive, especially by the twenty-five-pound bag.

Wine for Cooking

It is said that the better the wine, the better the dish. There are definite limitations to this principle. While a fine aged Chardonnay will certainly spruce up your fish stock, it will do your table even better. You might, though, in a moment of largesse or wealth, sacrifice a generous splash of that same jewel to the completion of a cream and white wine reduction and get a result almost worthy of the wine.

Here are a few rules of thumb concerning wine for cooking. The wine should almost always be dry, have at least medium body, and be young, with good solid acid content. In most cases there is no reason to spend a lot of money for it. For my taste, a good white wine for cooking is a young dry Chardonnay or a simple jug wine if the blend is not too heavy on the Semillon or Chenin Blanc grapes. For a red wine, I prefer a Zinfandel or, again, a dry red jug wine. For reductions of brown stock and red wine, especially on game or duck, nothing beats a young, robust, even coarse Zinfandel.

BASICS

TECHNIQUES
Buying and Storing Fish

Buying and storing fish are skills essential to any professional chef. The chef has a major advantage over the person shopping for the home table, because a day-to-day relationship with the supplier is carefully nurtured. The supplier understands the restaurant's needs and vice versa. The restaurant can always get fish that were bought that day at the wholesale market—fish that were, in most cases, caught only the day before, or even in the middle of the night.

The wholesale fish market is a rough place, and wholesalers do not hesitate to take advantage of the uninformed or careless buyer, which often means that a retailer may try to sell you his mistakes. A retailer also has to sell the fish left from the day before, which are sometimes just fine, although it is hard for the shopper to tell. So here are some guidelines.

1. When in doubt, ask. Which fish came in today? Tell the counterperson that your aged granny is allergic to seaborne bacteria and has to have the freshest fish or she'll die.

2. Learn to judge fish yourself. Through experience, it is possible to tell which fish are fresh on a given day and to estimate the approximate age of every fish in the counter. The freshest fish almost glow. Fish have a natural mucous coating, and this is what makes them shine when they are fresh. As the fish lies around in the walk-in or counter, the coating dries out and the fish looks dull. Do not go entirely by the appearance of the eyes. Fish are packed in crushed ice for shipping, and often the eyes freeze, causing them to appear dull. If the eyes are dull and sunken, though, that is an old fish. Go by the overall appearance of the fish and pay the most attention to the sheen of the fish. In buying fillets, which is what most domestic shoppers do, it is even harder to judge quality. The best rule is to go by the prettiness of the piece of fish. It should shine. It should beg you to buy it. You should think, "What a pretty piece of fish!"

3. Even though fish can be stored for up to five days, depending on the type of fish and its condition to start with, it is best to eat the fish the same day you buy it. If you must buy fish for tomorrow, wrap it tightly in plastic as soon as you get it home, and store it in the coldest place in your refrigerator (but not the freezer, silly). If you are storing whole fish, have the fish gutted and scaled, and, in either case, be extra demanding as to freshness.

Peeling and Using Garlic

In restaurants, large amounts of garlic are peeled at one time. The peeled garlic is stored in a container of oil and used as needed. It is important to seal garlic from contact with air as soon as it is peeled, because the flavor of garlic resides in certain volatile oils that oxidize on contact with the air, giving the garlic an acrid flavor.

You will find a wide range of garlic flavors used in this book. Because of the volatility of garlic's oils, different cooking techniques produce different flavors. Raw puréed garlic added to a dish at the last moment gives a strong, almost overpowering flavor, which is cherished in some dishes. At the other end of the scale is the sweet, subtle flavor of garlic that has been cooked for a long time at a low temperature, such as baked garlic or garlic simmered in a stock or stew. And in between we have the potent flavor of garlic browned in oil, and the rich flavor of garlic sautéed briefly and then simmered with the rest of a dish. As you can see, we have a lot of fun with garlic in Berkeley. Life here just wouldn't be the same without it.

To peel garlic restaurant style, remove the outer layers of loose parchmentlike stuff from a whole head of garlic. Put the head of garlic on its side on a hard surface, rest the heel of your right hand on it, cover your right hand with the left and lean forward, putting most of your weight on the head of garlic. It will separate into cloves. Next, with a kitchen mallet or the flat of a cleaver, crush the cloves lightly; they should be cracked open, not mashed flat. Pick up each clove by the pointed end, pinch it between your fingers, and, with your other hand, twist the clove out of its husk and drop it into a small container of oil. (You might as well peel another head; it keeps for weeks in the refrigerator.)

Grilling

This is one of the most important techniques used in Berkeley, arguably the most influential development in American cooking in years. Silly, of course—man has been burning his dinner over an open fire for eons. But it became newly popular here, and led to a style of simplicity in cooking that took off like a Chez Panisse mesquite shed on fire.

Fuels for Grilling

Mesquite is all the vogue for grilling, and for good reason. Commercial charcoal briquets may have the advantages of price and easier-to-control heat, but they impart a flavor of petroleum to the food, which is easy to understand since they are composed mostly of petroleum wastes. Mesquite burns with an intense heat, which is at times a blessing and at others a curse. It works beautifully for fish, but it can set a grill full of split chickens afire. The covered barbecue grill is the answer to this problem, for it allows the cook to control the amount of air the fire gets and therefore how much fire there is to be. *Gas* is another fuel used both in restaurants and at home, and while there is nothing wrong with it, there is also nothing to recommend it, as it adds no flavor of its own to the food.

The most underestimated fuel, in my opinion, is also the oldest: *wood*. It is the very definition of organic, has lots of character, and is no more expensive than charcoal—in fact it's often free. While it may take certain woodsmanly skills to kindle the fire, there is a primitive satisfaction in doing so.

While starting your charcoal or wood fire Boy Scout style does avoid the unpleasant and probably poisonous odors of charcoal lighter, there are at least two easier ways. One is with a chimney device that holds a few pieces of charcoal or wood. You wad up one piece of newspaper, place it underneath, light it, and the chimney funnels the heat through the fuel, igniting it rapidly. You then build your fire around those few lit pieces. The other method is an electric lighting coil, which you pile charcoal around and leave on for about 10 minutes. Both methods work well, and the chimney lighter is very inexpensive.

Roasting and Peeling Peppers

This is an age-old procedure. Roasting and peeling peppers greatly enhances their sweetness and mellows their flavors. While there are many techniques, the principles are the same: application of some kind of heat to the skin to loosen it from the meat, a period of steaming and cooling, then removal of the skin. The easiest method I know is to char the skin of the pepper over an open flame, either gas or charcoal. This takes about 5 minutes and should result in a pepper that is almost completely black (yes, black). The hot pepper is then put into a paper bag, which is folded closed, and the pepper is left to cool. The charred skin is either scraped or rinsed off (purists insist on scraping, maintaining that rinsing causes flavor loss), then the pepper is stemmed, seeded, and cut as desired, for most dishes into long narrow strips.

RECIPES

Beurre Blanc

Beurre blanc is one member of a large family of hot butter sauces. These sauces are formed by the emulsification of butterfat with the milk solids and water of butter by the action of a strongly acid, usually flavored, reduction. In practice what happens is that an acid liquid such as wine vinegar or lemon juice is reduced over medium heat with flavorings such as wine, shallots, or herbs to an almost syrupy consistency, just a tablespoon or so in volume. Then, over low heat, cold butter is melted into the reduction, whose very acid nature binds the fatty components with the watery elements of the butter, forming what is called an emulsion and which has an attractive, creamy appearance. Butter continues to be melted into the sauce until the acid balance tastes correct. The beginner should do this process over low heat, but the experienced professional can do it over a roaring flame.

Here is a basic beurre blanc recipe. Bear in mind that it can be flavored in any way desired, as long as the basic architecture of the sauce is honored.

¼ cup white wine vinegar
¼ cup fresh lemon juice
¼ cup dry white wine
2 tablespoons minced shallots
2 cups (4 sticks) cold unsalted butter, cut into 12 pieces

In a heavy, nonreactive saucepan (enameled or stainless steel), boil the shallots and liquids until only a tablespoon or so remains. Remove the saucepan from the heat and immediately stir in 2 pieces of cold butter. As the butter melts and is incorporated, return the pan to a low flame and add the rest of the butter a piece at a time, stirring constantly. As you approach the end of the butter, taste the sauce to make sure it will be neither too acid nor too bland. Once the sauce is complete, it may be kept in a very warm, but not hot, place for several hours.

If you do something wrong, such as using warm or melted butter or too much heat, and the sauce "breaks" or turns thin and oily, it may be recovered in one of two ways: Make a small amount of a new reduction, add more cold butter, and then add the broken sauce gradually to that, or whisk a small amount of the broken sauce in a mixing bowl with a small piece of ice, then work in the broken sauce. In my experience, the first method works more reliably.

To vary the sauce, add herbs to simmer with the reduction or after the sauce is complete. The sauce may be flavored with chopped fresh tomatoes, garlic, chilies, or spices. Or you may use all lemon juice and omit the vinegar, or use orange or another fruit juice. There are no limits so long as there is enough

acid to make the sauce hold together. Stocks may also be reduced along with the vinegar; fish stock and tarragon, for example, is a simple variation of the basic recipe.

Composed Butters

These are flavored butters. Good-quality unsalted butter is softened, and then a concentrated flavor of some kind is introduced, for instance a reduction of orange juice and garlic, or lime juice, lime zest, and ground coriander. The butter is then shaped as desired—usually into a roll about 2 inches in diameter—chilled, and served over hot grilled foods.

Stocks

Restaurants make extensive use of stocks, and so does this book. Stocks form the basis for so many flavors and techniques that a chef is lost without at least three on hand at all times. The making of stock is so simple that the recipe is almost just a concept: clean bones and leftovers simmered in water with or without flavorings until their essence is extracted. It should be remembered that stocks freeze well, can be made in large quantity, and require relatively little of the cook's time, so it is easy to guarantee that you will never be without them. (To store them in the refrigerator, bring to a boil every 3 or 4 days.) If you do get caught short, it is possible to buy stocks in some delicatessens. As a last resort, canned broths are available and can be made to resemble the real thing by simmering them with some carrots, celery, onions, etc., as well as whatever meat or fish scraps you may have around. Dehydrated bouillon cubes or soup bases do more harm than good. They have a phony flavor that no amount of adjusting can disguise.

The same rules apply to materials for stock as to ingredients in general: Freshness and cleanliness are paramount. We will discuss the three basic stocks: chicken stock, fish stock and brown stock. For *chicken (or duck) stock*, use bones, (raw or cooked), skin, fat, and leftover meat. Any one or any combination of these is fine. The raw components must be washed thoroughly. For *fish stock*, use bones, heads and meat only; never use the fins, tail, or skin. These contain oils that give stock a fishy taste. The parts for fish stock must be washed clean of all blood and slime, which usually takes three rinsings in cold water. For *brown stock*, use beef, veal, or pork bones and meat and scraps, or a mixture (brown poultry stock can be made with the same ingredients). Veal bones contain lots of gelatin, which gives the stock body and is important if the stock is to be reduced to a glaze. The material for brown stock can be trimmed of fat before cooking; this simplifies the skimming process. Bones for brown stock should not be washed, because this slows the browning process. In a large roasting pan, arrange the bones in one layer and roast them in a 500° oven until they are well browned, but not burned. This will take about an hour for beef bones, and about half an hour for poultry. With tongs, remove the bones to a large pot and pour off the grease from the roasting pan, reserving it if desired. Rinse out the pan and add the deglazing to the stock.

The simmering process is identical for all stocks, the only variable being cooking time.

Stock should be cooked in a large nonreactive pot; aluminum discolors it. Place the bones in the pot and add generous quantities of aromatic vegetables: onions, carrots, celery, parsley stems, garlic, and herbs. This is the point at which you can flavor the stock according to your intentions. The vegetables for brown stock can be used raw, browned with the bones, or sautéed. Cold water should be added to cover the stock material by at least 2 inches, and then the pot goes over a high flame. As it approaches boiling, blood and other impurities will begin to be cooked out and will rise to the surface as a foam. Hover resolutely over the pot for the next 10 minutes or so, skimming carefully with a large spoon or shallow ladle. Do not let the stock reach an actual boil. It should only simmer; that is, occasional bubbles will rise to the top. You should never stir a stock, but it is acceptable to jostle the bones gently to dislodge bits of scum that get hung up and don't float up to the surface. When the stock stops sending up foam, you are basically done skimming. An occasional visit to remove excess fat will be sufficient.

Cooking times vary. Fish stock is usually done in an hour or less. Chicken stock is best after 8 hours. A brown duck stock likes to cook about 24 hours, and a brown beef, veal, or lamb stock should really cook for 3 days. If you are in a hurry, cook the stock as long as you can and then call it done. Let the stock cool in the pot, then ladle it out through a strainer lined with layers of cheesecloth or a kitchen towel, and finally pour out the last liquid from the pot when it gets too far down to use the ladle.   PTJ

Compliments of the Chef

100 Great Recipes from the Innovative Restaurants & Cafes of Berkeley, California

For years a Berkeley standby in the realm of classic French cooking, A La Carte was one of the first restaurants in town to offer an à la carte menu allowing diners to compose their own meal according to taste and budget. Located near an unlikely corner in a residential neighborhood, this tiny restaurant, with its enormous fireplace, ornate plasterwork, and starched pink linens, conveys a feeling of quiet intimacy.

Compliments of

A LA CARTE
BERKELEY

Suprême de Volaille en Feuilletée

Chicken Breast in Puff Pastry

This rich main dish is a bit tricky; if your pastry does not puff using the technique given here, try using a crêpe as a base for the stuffed chicken breast and folding the puff pastry over all.

½ cup *each* minced fresh chives and dill
½ cup minced fresh dill
1 cup minced fresh parsley
½ cup chopped fresh chervil
¼ cup chopped garlic
1½ pounds natural cream cheese
Salt and pepper
2 pounds puff pastry
8 whole chicken breasts, skinned and boned
  but left whole
1 egg yolk mixed with
1 tablespoon heavy cream

Cream the herbs and garlic together with the cream cheese. Season to taste with salt and pepper and set aside. Roll out the puff pastry ¼ to ⅛ inch thick. Cut into eight 6- by 10-inch rectangles. Place approximately 3 tablespoons of the herbed cream cheese filling on each breast and fold the meat over it, taking care not to overfill.

Place the filled breast on a piece of pastry and fold the pastry over the meat loosely so that it will have room to puff. Seal the edges, chill for 1 hour, and place seam side down and well apart on an ungreased cookie sheet. Brush with the egg-cream mixture. Bake in a preheated 400° oven for 20 to 30 minutes, or until golden brown. *Serves 8.*

Pots de Crème au Chocolat Grand Marnier

Chocolate Custard Cream

A rich and satisfying dessert, easy to execute.

2⅔ cups plus ½ cup heavy cream
8 ounces (8 squares) fine bittersweet baking
  chocolate
8 large egg yolks
8 tablespoons sugar
1 tablespoon vanilla extract
¼ cup plus dash Grand Marnier
Powdered sugar
Chocolate shavings (optional)

Pour 2⅔ cups of the cream into a heavy saucepan over low heat. Add the chocolate and melt, stirring occasionally; do not boil. In a large bowl, beat the egg yolks into the sugar with a whisk until well mixed. Slowly, to avoid scrambling the yolks, pour the chocolate-cream mixture into the egg-sugar mixture, whisking to blend well. Add the vanilla and ¼ cup of the Grand Marnier and mix well.

Pour into 8 ungreased 4-ounce custard cups and place in a roasting pan with ½ inch of water covering the bottom. Bake in a preheated 200° oven for 1 hour, or until the top is slightly firm to the touch (your finger should not leave an imprint). Chill 1 hour.

To serve, whip the remaining ½ cup cream with a sprinkle of powdered sugar and a dash of Grand Marnier. Place a spoonful on top of each custard and add chocolate shavings, if desired. *Serves 8.*

A focus on pasta and grilled fish is the hallmark of this restaurant. Grilled foods are accompanied with simple sauces, the pasta and seafood are absolutely fresh, and the menu changes daily. Owner Bonnie Hughes has managed to incorporate a Continental flavor into quintessential California cuisine. Displays of antipasti and desserts greet diners as they enter the lower dining room, where tables are arranged around a central fireplace. The partially open kitchen dominates the upper, more casual dining room, with a large enclosed garden dining area beyond.

Once a year Augusta's presents an entire meal devoted to "unmentionable cuisine" including, among other offerings, snake and conch. Although the less adventurous may choose to forego this experience, enthusiastic diners have included food writers and cooks from all over California.

Compliments of

AUGUSTA'S
BERKELEY

Caesar Salad

One of the best renditions of a popular Berkeley salad. A meal by itself on a hot summer day, it is also an ideal beginner for a menu based on grilled food. Always use freshly grated Parmesan cheese for a Caesar salad, Reggiano if possible.

Croutons

½-inch-thick slices of day-old French bread or
   quarter-inch slices of day-old baguette,
   cubed (enough to make ¾ cups of croutons)
Olive oil
1 or 2 garlic cloves, minced

2 eggs
1 large head romaine lettuce
3 tablespoons fresh lemon juice, or more to
   taste
¾ cup olive oil
1 garlic clove, minced
¼ teaspoon Worcestershire sauce
2 tablespoons chopped anchovies
⅓ cup freshly grated Parmesan cheese

Prepare croutons by toasting the cubed bread in a preheated 300° oven for 30 minutes, or until lightly brown and completely dry. Drizzle with olive oil and some minced garlic and toast another 5 minutes. Set aside. (These will keep for several days in a sealed container. Do not refrigerate.)

   Coddle the 2 eggs in boiling water for 30 seconds. Tear the lettuce into bite-sized pieces. Beat the eggs well. Combine the lemon juice, oil, and garlic and mix well. Gradually whisk in the eggs, forming an emulsion. Add the Worcestershire and anchovies. Toss with the lettuce, Parmesan, and croutons. Garnish with additional Parmesan if desired. *Serves 2 to 4.*

Roast Garlic Potatoes

This simple and very popular dish is an obvious choice to serve with steaks, roasts, or any other uncomplicated dish. The amount of garlic may be adjusted to your taste, and olive oil is a good substitute for clarified butter. Other types of potatoes also work well. After baking, the garlic becomes soft and sweet and is squeezed out of the husk to flavor each bite of potato.

4 medium russet potatoes
Salt and ground white pepper to taste
24 whole unpeeled garlic cloves
   (less or more if desired)
½ cup clarified butter or olive oil

Cut the potatoes in half and then cut each half into thirds. Put the potatoes, skin side down, in an oiled baking pan. Sprinkle with salt and white pepper. Add the whole cloves of garlic (with their skins) on top of the potatoes. Drizzle the clarified butter or olive oil on top. Bake in a preheated 375° oven for 30 to 45 minutes. To prepare ahead, reheat at 450° for 10 minutes. They will be brown, slightly puffed, and ready to serve immediately; they will not wait. *Serves 4.*

Tomato, Basil, and Pine Nut Fettuccine

A pasta that is easy on the cook, and great for a quick meal or as a first course in an elaborate menu. Roasting the tomatoes dries them out and gives them a special flavor. Roma, or plum, tomatoes work best because of their lower moisture content.

3 tablespoons pine nuts
2 pounds tomatoes, cored and cut into
   wedges
3 tablespoons olive oil
Salt and pepper to taste
Small handful basil leaves
2 tablespoons minced garlic
¼ cup white wine
¼ cup chicken stock
½ tablespoon dried red pepper flakes
½ pound fresh pasta
Freshly grated Parmesan

Toast the pine nuts for 10 minutes in a preheated 300° oven. Roast the tomatoes in a 400° oven with 1 tablespoon of the olive oil, salt, and pepper, until the skins are slightly browned. Chop the basil coarsely. Sauté the garlic in the remaining 2 tablespoons of olive oil. Add the tomatoes, pine nuts, and basil. Add the wine and stock and cook until slightly reduced. Season with red pepper flakes.

Cook the pasta in lots of salted boiling water until *al dente*, 2 to 3 minutes. Mix a little sauce into the freshly cooked pasta and pour the rest over the top. Serve with grated Parmesan. *Serves 4.*

Sautéed Swordfish with Tomato and Dill Sauce

Sautéed swordfish with tomato and dill sauce is a quick and easy dish. Fresh dill makes all the difference here. Sweet cream may be used instead of crème fraîche, but a few drops of lemon juice should be added to simulate the tang of crème fraîche.

2 swordfish steaks, 6 to 8 ounces each
1 tablespoon clarified butter
1 teaspoon minced garlic
1 tablespoon peeled, seeded, and chopped
   tomato
¼ cup dry white wine
½ cup crème fraîche
1 teaspoon chopped fresh dill
4 tablespoons butter
Salt and pepper
Lemon wedges
Sprigs of dill

In a sauté pan or skillet, gently sauté the swordfish in the clarified butter until just done, about 3 to 5 minutes per side, depending on the thickness of the steaks (the fish should be slightly translucent in the center). Remove from the pan and keep warm.

Add the garlic, tomato, and wine to the pan and reduce until almost dry. Add the crème fraîche and reduce by one-third to one-half. Remove from the heat. Add the dill. Add the butter, stirring until it melts and is incorporated into the sauce. Season to taste with salt and pepper and pour over the swordfish. Garnish with lemon wedges and dill. *Serves 2.*

For a restaurant that began as a cheese shop and cafe, the Bay Wolf has come far. It was created by former academics Michael Wild, Larry Goldman, and Michael Phelps (the name of the restaurant is a literary pun). Now Wild and Carol Brendlinger have developed the Bay Wolf into one of the most respected restaurants in the Bay Area. It is located in a Victorian house with detailed woodwork, etched glass, and a handsome bar. A large outdoor dining deck overlooks the busy scene on Piedmont Avenue.

The Bay Wolf features an eclectic French menu that changes daily, and even the most frequent patrons are unlikely to anticipate some of the imaginative combinations devised in this kitchen. Michael Wild, harking back to his childhood in Provençe, has evolved a unique style of California cuisine based on French country cooking modified by Creole and Mideastern influences. The management of the Bay Wolf is also unusual: many of the decisions are made by the staff, and this group participation is reflected in the high quality of the food and friendliness of the service.

Giblet Soup with Barley, Garlic, and Mushrooms

A robust soup, created by Michael Wild, that could stand alone as a meal or could serve to introduce a roast of fowl. If you plan to serve it the following day, have some stock on hand to dilute it, as the barley soaks up moisture over time.

2 ounces dried *porcini* mushrooms
1 quart poultry stock
Salt to taste
⅓ cup barley
1 garlic clove, chopped
1 pound giblets, trimmed and finely diced
¾ pound fresh mushrooms, domestic or
    wild
1 garlic clove, minced
2 celery stalks, minced
1 medium onion, minced
3 green onions, sliced thin
6 parsley sprigs, chopped
4 tablespoons peanut oil or rendered chicken,
    duck, or goose fat

Gremolata

6 garlic cloves
1 bunch parsley
Zest of 2 lemons

Soak the porcini in hot water to cover for 1 hour; drain the mushrooms, reserving the soaking liquid. Place the poultry stock in a large saucepan, salt lightly, add the barley, and simmer about 45 minutes, or until tender. Add the chopped garlic to the broth. In a large, heavy pot, sauté the giblets, fresh mushrooms, garlic, celery, onions, and parsley in the oil until pleasantly aromatic and nearly tender. Add the cooked barley and stock and mushroom soaking liquid; simmer for 15 minutes.

Prepare the *gremolata* by mincing the garlic, parsley, and lemon zest together with a chef's knife or in a food processor. Serve the soup with the gremolata on the side. *Serves 4 to 6.*

Spinach Salad with Duck Cracklings

This recipe came from a menu by Michael Wild, which used a different part of the duck for every course of the meal, except dessert. Duck cracklings make this an interesting and successful variation of spinach salad.

Skin from 3 duck breasts
1 lemon cucumber or English or Japanese
    cucumber
2 bunches spinach leaves, stemmed
⅓ cup grape juice or Gamay verjuice
2 tablespoons fresh lemon juice
⅜ cup olive oil
1 shallot, minced
Salt and pepper to taste

Place the duck skin on a rack in a pan in a preheated 375° oven for 45 minutes, or until the skin is crisp and browned, but not too brown. (A convection oven works well for this.) Save the fat for other cooking. Crack the skin into small pieces and drain on paper towels.

Peel, seed, and julienne the cucumber. Add to the spinach and toss with a dressing made by combining the grape juice or verjuice, lemon juice, olive oil, shallot, salt, and pepper. Sprinkle the salad with the cracklings and serve immediately. *Serves 4 to 6.*

Pumpkin Ravioli with Crème Fraîche and Chives

An unusual first course for an elaborate meal or a main course for a simple one, these raviolis, created by Carol Brendlinger, lend themselves beautifully to variation. The simple addition of a variety of fresh herbs to the pumpkin purée makes an already excellent dish even more interesting. Favorite additions are mint, marjoram, and basil. Imagination, discretion, and the rest of the menu are the only limitations.

Canned pumpkin can be used, but fresh is better. To cook it, steam or bake peeled pumpkin slices until tender and drain well to prevent the filling from being too wet. If pumpkin is not available, use butternut squash or another winter squash. The raviolis do not hold or freeze well, as they tend to stick together. And take care with the sauce, which curdles easily (although it will still taste fine).

Filling

1 cup fresh pumpkin purée, well drained
1 egg, beaten
¼ pound cheese (grated Gruyère or Parmesan, or crumbled *chèvre*)

¼ cup minced fresh chives
¼ teaspoon salt
¼ teaspoon ground white pepper

½ pound fresh pasta cut into 4-inch-wide sheets.

Sauce

2 cups *crème fraîche*
4 egg yolks
½ teaspoon grated lemon zest
¼ teaspoon salt
Pinch of ground white pepper
¼ cup minced fresh chives

Mix the ingredients for the filling together. Make a row of teaspoonfuls of the filling 2 inches apart along one side of the pasta sheets. Fold each sheet in half lengthwise, moistening the dough around the filling with water to make it stick together. Press to seal, pushing out any air bubbles. Cut into squares with a ravioli wheel. Cook in a large amount of boiling salted water for 2 to 5 minutes (depending on thickness of pasta) or until *al dente*.

Meanwhile, prepare the sauce by mixing all the sauce ingredients in the top of a double boiler. Heat slowly over simmering water, whisking constantly, until the sauce thickens. Drain the ravioli in a colander. Pour the sauce over the ravioli and serve immediately. *Serves 6 as a main course, 12 as an appetizer.*

Duck Sausage Wrapped in Grape Leaves with Zinfandel Sauce

Another magnificent dish from Bay Wolf's all-duck menu is this most unusual sausage, involving neither pork nor sausage casing. A meat grinder is preferable to a food processor for this recipe because the processor cannot cut the tendinous material that runs through the meat of the duck leg.

Four-spices, or quatre-épices, is a blend of one part each clove, nutmeg, and ginger to three parts cinnamon (you can substitute allspice).

Sausage

Fresh or canned grape leaves
6 boned duck legs, uncooked
1 shallot
2 to 3 garlic cloves
Salt and pepper to taste
⅓ teaspoon four-spices (see introductory note)
Pinch dried red pepper flakes
1 cup duck stock or rich chicken stock

Sauce

2 quarts duck stock or rich chicken stock
Reserved braising liquid
1 bottle Zinfandel

If the grape leaves are fresh, blanch first in salted water for 10 minutes before wrapping. Put the duck meat through a meat grinder with the shallot, garlic, and spices. Mix well,

divide into 12 portions, and wrap in the grape leaves. Pour the duck or chicken stock into a pan large enough to hold all of the sausages. Braise in a preheated 400° oven for 30 minutes or cook on a covered charcoal grill. In either case, reserve the braising liquid to use in the sauce.

To make the sauce, combine the stock and Zinfandel in a pan and reduce to a syrupy sauce. (You can flavor the reduction, if you like, with tomato, garlic, onion, thyme, *herbes de Provence*, and small amounts of celery and carrot.) Pour the sauce over the sausage. Garnish with polenta that has been cooked, cooled in a flat pan, cut into shapes with a cookie cutter, and grilled or sautéed. *Serves 6 as an entrée, 10 to 12 as an appetizer.*

BETTE'S OCEANVIEW DINER

BERKELEY

For those of us who remember, entering Bette's is like stepping into a '57 Chevy Bel Air. Bette's is a lively eighties version of a fifties diner, complete with jukebox, rotating counter stools covered in vinyl, clean-lined chrome trim, and Fiestaware crockery. The updated American menu features some Mexican influences, and the food is both hearty and imaginative. The crowd is diverse, and on any visit you are likely to encounter exercise buffs from the studio next door as well as businessmen in three-piece suits enjoying the excellent food and upbeat atmosphere.

Huevos Rancheros

Ranch-Style Eggs

What more could you want for breakfast than spicy beans, tortillas, and fried eggs topped with melted cheese and salsa? Make sure to cook the beans long enough so that they begin to melt into a creamy purée, adding water as needed to prevent scorching. The sauce and bean recipes make enough for six to eight servings; the Huevos Rancheros recipe instructions are for one serving.

2 eggs
Butter for frying
½ cup Salsa, following
¼ cup shredded Cheddar cheese
¼ cup shredded jack cheese
1 flour tortilla
Black Beans, following
1 tablespoon sour cream

In a small shallow ovenproof pan, cook the eggs sunnyside up in a little butter until set on bottom but loose on top. Spoon ¼ cup salsa onto the eggs and top with shredded Cheddar and jack cheese to cover. Place the pan under the broiler until the cheese melts. Warm a flour tortilla in a sauté pan or skillet in a little butter. Slide the eggs onto the tortilla. Serve immediately with black beans topped with the remaining salsa and the sour cream. Serves 1.

Black Beans

1 pound dried black beans
1 medium yellow onion, minced
1 tablespoon ground cumin
1 tablespoon ground coriander
½ teaspoon cayenne
2 tablespoons olive oil
2 garlic cloves, minced
½ cup fresh orange juice
1 tablespoon salt
Ground pepper to taste

Soak the beans overnight in water to cover. In a sauté pan or skillet, sauté the onion, cumin, coriander, and cayenne in the olive oil until the onions are translucent. Add water to 2 inches above the surface of the beans. Combine the water and beans with the onion mixture in a heavy pot and simmer, uncovered, until the beans are soft and a thick sauce forms, about 2 hours. Add the garlic, orange juice, salt, pepper, and more water if necessary. Simmer another 30 minutes, stirring. Makes about 6 cups

Salsa

6 to 8 ripe tomatoes, diced
1 bunch green onions, minced
2 fresh jalapeño peppers, diced
   (for a milder dish, stem and seed the
   peppers)
1 tablespoon salt
2 shakes Tabasco sauce
2 tablespoons butter

Simmer the tomatoes, green onions, jalapeños, salt, Tabasco, and butter in a saucepan until the liquid is reduced and the tomatoes have cooked down to the consistency of a loose purée. Makes 3 to 4 cups.
   NOTE: This sauce will keep in the refrigerator for about a week.

German-Style
Potato Pancakes

These pancakes are versatile enough to be served as a side dish for most meats, and they are excellent for breakfast as well.

1 small onion, grated
2 eggs, well beaten
¼ cup unbleached all-purpose flour
Salt and pepper to taste
6 medium russet potatoes, peeled
Shortening

Combine the grated onion, eggs, flour, salt, and pepper in a large mixing bowl and beat until the batter is smooth. Shred the potatoes on the big holes of a hand grater. Squeeze the potatoes in a clean tea towel until they are as dry as possible. Add the potatoes to the batter.

In a large sauté pan or skillet, melt shortening to the depth of ¼ inch. When it is hot but not smoking, spoon in mounds of potatoes and flatten into pancakes with the back of a spatula. When the pancakes are golden brown on the bottom, turn and press with the spatula again. Cook until golden brown and crisp. Remove from the pan with a slotted spatula and drain on paper towels. Serve hot with applesauce, sour cream, jam or sugar. *Serves 6.*

Souffléed
Apple Pancake

This is just the dish for a special brunch, and it would make a nice dessert with the addition of a little more sugar and a fruit sauce. The apples can be replaced by bananas, berries, or other fruits in season.

2 green apples
4 tablespoons butter
¼ teaspoon ground cinnamon
2 teaspoons sugar
¾ cup half and half
½ cup unbleached all-purpose flour
¼ teaspoon salt
3 eggs, separated
4 tablespoons melted butter
2 tablespoons rum or brandy

Peel and slice the apples. In a sauté pan or skillet, sauté the apple slices lightly in 2 tablespoons of the butter, and add the cinnamon and sugar. Set aside. Combine the half and half, flour, and salt in a mixing bowl. Beat the egg yolks lightly and add to batter, then add the melted butter and the rum or brandy. Beat the egg whites until they form soft peaks. Fold the batter into them.

In an ovenproof skillet, heat the remaining 2 tablespoons of butter until it foams. Add the batter and cook briefly over medium heat. Arrange the apples on the top and continue cooking until the bottom is golden brown and bubbles form around the edge of the pancake. Place the pan under a preheated broiler until the middle is firm and the top is golden brown and puffed. *Serves 2.*

*D*avid Morris's motivation for opening his bakery typifies an honored tradition in Berkeley: "to make a living doing the thing I most enjoy. . ." Drawing on traditional European recipes, he bakes unusual and authentic breads. He also has the distinction of being one of the first bakers in Berkeley to produce what is now a local staple, the handmade baguette. On Sunday mornings long lines form outside his small storefront, as patrons wait patiently to approach the trays of still-warm bread and rolls.

Compliments of

BREAD GARDEN
BERKELEY

German Potato Bread

German potato bread is a light-colored, chewy loaf with a dense texture. It is simple to make, muscle-building to knead, and can be ready to eat within three hours.

1 package (1 tablespoon) dry yeast
1½ cups lukewarm water (150° to 115°)
1 cup mashed cooked potatoes, cooled
1 tablespoon vegetable oil
2 teaspoons salt
5 to 6 cups unbleached all-purpose flour
1 egg mixed with
2 tablespoons water
Poppy seeds

Dissolve the yeast in the water in a large bowl for 5 to 10 minutes. Add the potatoes, oil, salt, and 2 cups of the flour. Stir until well blended, then start adding more flour until the dough is quite stiff. Turn the dough out onto a lightly floured surface and knead for 10 minutes, working in more flour until at least 5 cups (but not more than 6) of the flour have been incorporated into the dough. When the kneading is done, the dough should be stiffer than usual bread dough. It will soften while rising. Cover and let rise in a warm place until doubled in size, about 1 hour.

Preheat the oven to 375°. Divide the dough into 2 pieces and shape each like a potato. Place the loaves on a greased baking sheet and cut a 1-inch-deep slit lengthwise down each loaf. Brush the loaf with the egg and water, then liberally dust the loaves with poppy seeds. Place a pan of hot water on the lower rack of the oven, and immediately place the loaves in the oven. Bake for 1 hour, or until no white spots remain on the crust. *Makes 2 loaves.*

NOTE: Unlike most breads, this bread is not allowed to rise again after shaping. This adds to the chewiness of the loaf.

Cinnamon-Swirl Loaves

A fragrant, sweet bread to serve with a fruit salad or to toast as a breakfast bread. This is also a good bread for French toast.

1 package (1 tablespoon) dry yeast
2 cups lukewarm water (105° to 115°)
¾ cup dried instant milk powder
½ cup sugar
7 to 8 cups unbleached all-purpose flour
½ cup oil or melted butter
2 teaspoons salt
2 eggs, lightly beaten
1 egg, mixed with
¼ cup water
¾ cup sugar, mixed with
3 tablespoons ground cinnamon

In a large bowl, dissolve the yeast in the water for 5 to 10 minutes. Stir in the dried milk, sugar, 4 to 5 cups of the flour, oil or melted butter, salt, and 2 beaten eggs. Mix well. Stir in the rest of the flour cup by cup (using as little as possible) until the dough pulls away from the side of the bowl. Turn out onto a lightly floured surface and knead at least 10 minutes, using as little as possible of the remaining flour to keep the dough from sticking. Cover with a clean cloth or plastic wrap and let rise in a warm place until doubled in size, about 1 hour.

After the dough has risen, divide it into 2 equal pieces. Using a rolling pin, roll out each half into a 15-by-7-inch rectangle. Paint each rectangle with the egg-water mixture, then sprinkle each with half of the cinnamon-sugar mixture, leaving 1 inch of one of the short ends of each rectangle uncovered. Roll the rectangles jelly-roll style towards the uncovered edge (the finished rolls will be 7 inches wide) and place each seam side down in an oiled bread pan. Cover the loaves and let rise until doubled, about 1 hour. Brush the tops of the loaves with the remaining egg-water mixture and bake in a preheated 350° oven for 40 minutes. When the loaves are done, they will sound hollow when removed from the pan and tapped on the bottom. *Makes 2 loaves.*

Sticky Buns

The same dough used for Cinnamon-Swirl Loaves can be used to make sticky buns—or you can divide the bread recipe in half to make twelve buns and one loaf of bread.

Dough for Cinnamon Swirl Loaves, preceding
1 egg, mixed with
¼ cup water
¾ cup sugar, mixed with
3 tablespoons ground cinnamon
1½ cups raisins
½ cup dark brown sugar

After the dough has risen, roll it out into 1 large rectangle 20 inches by 10 inches. Brush the entire rectangle with the egg-water mixture and cover all but a 1-inch edge of the 20-inch side with the cinnamon-sugar mixture. Then sprinkle the raisins generously over the cinnamon-sugar mixture. Roll up the rectangle jelly-roll style towards the uncovered edge and cut into 24 equal pieces.

Oil four 8-inch round cake pans and place the brown sugar evenly over the bottom of each pan. Place 6 pieces of dough in each pan, let rise in a warm place until doubled in size, and bake in a preheated 350° oven for 30 minutes (until tops are nicely browned). Immediately after removing the pans from the oven, run a knife around the edge of the buns, remove from the pans, and invert them on cooling racks. Caution: Be careful not to burn yourself on the hot, runny brown sugar. *Makes 24 sticky buns.*

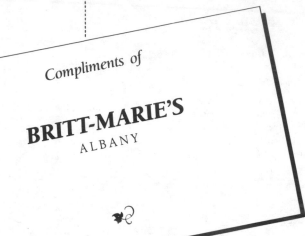

Compliments of

BRITT-MARIE'S
ALBANY

Jan and Britt-Marie Pazdirek have brought their Czechoslovakian and Swedish backgrounds and culinary skills to this small storefront restaurant. The dimmed lights and dark-wood wine bar create a European-cafe atmosphere. The menu, featuring late-night offerings in addition to full dinners, combines Eastern and Northern European dishes and desserts based on Britt-Marie's mother's Swedish recipes. The frequent use of garlic is also a hallmark of Britt-Marie's, and the 1984 Berkeley Garlic Festival gave the restaurant its Chef d'Ail award in recognition of the restaurant's dedication to the bulb.

Roasted Peppers with Creamed Feta

This is a simple and delightful appetizer, un-complicated and convenient in that it can be prepared well ahead of serving. If made in larger quantities with several kinds of peppers—red, yellow, green—the plate becomes most colorful.

1 bell pepper (red, yellow, or green)
3 garlic cloves
¼ cup olive oil
½ cup feta cheese
Cilantro leaves to taste

Roast, peel, seed, and julienne the pepper (see Basics). Sauté the garlic cloves in the olive oil until light gold. While still hot, pour the oil and garlic over the pepper strips. In a mixer or food processor, cream the feta with the cilantro leaves. Add a few drops of olive oil if the mixture is too dense. Serve at room temperature with Topinka (following), with the pepper strips arranged around the cheese.
Makes 2 servings.

Topinka

Another simple, satisfying appetizer to serve alone, or with Roasted Peppers with Creamed Feta, preceding.

1 slice rye bread, preferably 1 day old
Olive oil (optional)
1 garlic clove, cut in half, or puréed
  (use a garlic press) and mixed with
  1 teaspoon olive oil
Salt to taste
3 very thin slices Emmenthaler cheese
Hungarian paprika

Sauté the bread in a small amount of olive oil or toast it. While still hot, rub the bread with the garlic clove or spread with garlic-oil purée, sprinkle it with salt, and top with the cheese. Dust with paprika and serve immediately.
Makes 1 serving.

Czech Bread

This peasant bread is even heartier if you use whole-wheat flour rather than white flour. The potato makes for a chewier loaf. This is the bread to use for Topinka, preceding.

2 cups lukewarm water (105° to 115°)
1 package (1 tablespoon) dry yeast
2½ teaspoons salt
1 tablespoon caraway seeds
1 medium-sized potato, cooked, peeled, and grated
2 cups rye flour and 6 cups whole-wheat flour, *or* 8 cups unbleached all-purpose flour, *or* a mixture of white and rye flours totaling 8 cups

Mix the water, yeast, salt, caraway seeds, potato, and 4 cups of the flour in a large bowl. Stir well to blend, incorporating the flour little by little. *Do not knead* at this stage. Place in an oiled bowl and let rise in a warm place for approximately 1 hour, or until the dough is doubled in volume. Punch the dough down and mix in the remaining flour until the dough no longer sticks to the bowl. Turn the dough out onto a lightly floured surface. Knead the dough until all the flour is incorporated, and shape into 2 loaves. Slash the surface of the loaves diagonally with a sharp knife. Let rise in a warm place on a baking sheet that has been oiled or lined with parchment, until bread is doubled, about 1 hour.

The dough is ready to bake when you gently poke it with your finger and it doesn't spring back. Just before the loaves go into the oven, brush them with tepid water.

Bake in a preheated 450° oven for 15 minutes, or until the loaves are a golden color. Reduce the temperature to 300° and bake for another 45 minutes to 1 hour or until the loaves sound hollow when removed from the pans and tapped on the bottom. Remove the bread from the pans and cool on a rack. *Makes 2 loaves.*

Pear Tart

With the best-quality pears, this is a dessert that can't fail to please. The mock puff pastry makes a splendid shell and is well worth the time and effort involved.

Tart Dough

1¾ cups pastry flour or unbleached all-purpose flour
7 tablespoons cold unsalted butter, cut into small pieces
2 to 3 tablespoons water or heavy cream

Filling

3 juicy ripe pears, about 1 pound
¼ cup sour cream
¼ cup heavy cream
4 tablespoons sugar
2 tablespoons orange liqueur

Whipped unsweetened heavy cream

Sift the flour into a mixing bowl. Add the butter pieces, rubbing them into the flour with your fingertips or cutting them in with 2 knives or a pastry blender. Work the butter in for about a minute, or until the mixture looks like bread crumbs. Add just enough cold water to made the crumbs cohere in a mass. Work the dough with your hands until it is smooth and comes cleanly away from the sides of the bowl. Shape the dough into a ball, wrap in plastic wrap or foil, and refrigerate for at least 15 minutes to allow the dough to relax and the butter to become firm.

On a floured board, roll the dough into a rectangle about ¼ inch thick and 3 times as long as it is wide. Fold over one-third of the length of the rectangle; then fold over the remaining third. Wrap and chill the dough to firm it once more. Roll the dough into a rectangle again and fold as before. Chill again. Repeat rolling and turning once more. After the final turn, refrigerate for at least 1 hour before using. Tightly wrapped dough can safely be kept in the refrigerator for 2 or 3 days, or in the freezer for 2 months. If frozen, defrost it in the refrigerator overnight.

Roll the dough into a circle about ⅛ inch thick. Roll the dough onto the rolling pin, lift it up, and unroll it over a 10-inch tart pan. Press the dough firmly against the bottom and sides of the pan. Roll the pin across the top to cut off the excess dough around the rim. Prick the bottom with a fork. Chill the dough in the tart pan until firm in order to prevent shrinkage. Place aluminum foil filled with uncooked rice or beans on the bottom of the crust and bake in a preheated 350° oven until the crust is light golden.

Peel, halve, and core the pears. Cut the halves lengthwise into thin slices. Arrange the pear slices in overlapping rows on the prebaked tart shell. Mix the sour cream and heavy cream with the sugar and liqueur. Pour the mixture over the pear slices.

Bake in a preheated 400° oven for 10 to 15 minutes, or until the top is golden. Serve warm or at room temperature, garnished with whipped unsweetened cream. *Makes one 10-inch tart.*

NOTE: The hurried baker can skip the folding of the dough and still create a delicious tart, although the pastry will not be flaky. For a perfectly light and tender pastry: (1) keep the ingredients cold; (2) handle the dough as little and as rapidly as possible.

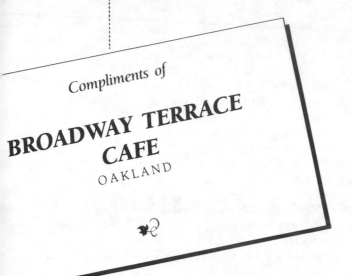

Compliments of

BROADWAY TERRACE CAFE
OAKLAND

Owner Albert Katz supervises and helps to cook a changing menu of astonishing variety and depth. His lighter touch in saucing mesquite-grilled foods has created a special place for the Broadway Terrace among East Bay grill restaurants. Although it is a relative newcomer, it is already very popular, demonstrating the value of professionalism and the importance of owner involvement in every aspect of the business. A former restaurant manager and consultant with a degree in business administration, Katz decided to drop out of the large-restaurant business and to apply his remarkable skills to his own personal vision. The result: a small restaurant consisting of several intimate dining areas, tucked away in a wooded residential section of the Oakland Hills.

Gorgonzola-Pear Salad

One of the most delicious salads around, this is a good way to begin or end any meal. Use a Gorgonzola that is crumbly rather than creamy, or your favorite blue cheese. It is also possible to substitute a sweet vinegar such as balsamic or another well-aged, mellow vinegar. Walnut oil is available from gourmet grocers.

The quality of the pears is crucial to this salad. They should be ripe, sweet, and creamy in texture—never mushy.

1 head romaine lettuce
¾ cup whole walnuts

Walnut Oil Vinaigrette

¼ cup reserved toasted walnuts
½ garlic clove
1 tablespoon red wine vinegar and
  1 tablespoon raspberry vinegar,
  or 2 tablespoons balsamic vinegar
Salt and pepper
3 tablespoons walnut oil
3 tablespoons light vegetable oil

½ cup crumbled Gorgonzola (domestic Tolibia
  if possible)
2 pears (red D'Anjou if possible), cored and
  cut lengthwise in eighths
½ bunch watercress

Separate the lettuce leaves, discarding the outer ones. Toast the walnuts in a preheated 325° oven for 5 minutes. Prepare a vinaigrette by puréeing ¼ cup of the toasted walnuts and the garlic. Add the vinegars and salt and pep-

per While slowly stirring, add the oils to emulsify.

Lay out the whole romaine leaves in a bowl and toss with the remaining ½ cup toasted walnuts, ½ cup of vinaigrette, and Gorgonzola and set on 4 serving plates. Top with pear slices and watercress and add any Gorgonzola left in the mixing bowl. *Serves 4.*

Fresh Corn Timbale
with Red Pepper Vinaigrette

We made this recipe twice during the testing just because we liked it so much. This type of recipe is characteristic of the Berkeley style of cooking in that it is a classic concept adapted to local ingredients and taste, with the addition of something unique—in this case a vinaigrette based on roasted red peppers (which could also be used for salads or on grilled fish).

2 ears corn
⅓ cup heavy cream
⅔ cup half and half
1 teaspoon sugar
2 eggs
1 egg yolk
Salt and ground white pepper to taste
Red Pepper Vinaigrette, following

Steam the corn for 5 minutes or until tender. Scrape the kernels off and put into a blender or food processor with the heavy cream. Purée until smooth.

Heat the half and half in a pan with the sugar until just scalded. Remove from the heat and add the puréed corn; let steep for a few minutes.

Beat the eggs and yolk together in a mixing bowl. Put the corn-cream mixture into a sieve and strain into the bowl, pressing with a rubber spatula to extract the juices, or use a food mill. Add the salt and white pepper.

Butter six 3-ounce timbale molds, fill, and place them in a roasting pan. Pour boiling water into the pan to halfway up the molds. Bake in a preheated 375° oven for 20 to 25 minutes, or until firm, lightly browned on top, and slightly puffed. Unmold onto a plate and surround with red pepper vinaigrette. *Serves 6.*

Red Pepper Vinaigrette

3 large red bell peppers
1 teaspoon chopped shallot
¼ teaspoon chopped garlic
1 tablespoon Dijon mustard
⅓ cup champagne vinegar or white wine
    vinegar*
¼ teaspoon salt
Pinch of ground white pepper and cayenne
¾ cup plus 2 tablespoons good olive oil

Roast, peel, seed, and chop the peppers (see Basics). In a blender or food processor, combine the shallot, garlic, mustard, vinegar, salt, white pepper, and cayenne. Slowly add the olive oil until the mixture thickens. With the machine running, add the roasted peppers. Taste and adjust seasonings. *Serves 6.*

*Use 5 percent acidity vinegar. Some champagne vinegars are 7 percent and too tart.

Four Sauces for Grilled Fish

These sauces are for simply cooked fish: grilled, poached or sautéed. In the best of the developing tradition of California cooking, these gems are straightforward, rely on seasonal components, and manage to unite seemingly disparate elements. Each sauce recipe is followed by a recommendation for the fish it should accompany, but don't be shy about combining any of the sauces with the best fish you can find at the time. You might even want to try some of them with a simply cooked meat.

Orange-Thyme Butter

1½ cups fresh orange juice
½ teaspoon chopped shallot
1 cup (2 sticks) unsalted butter, softened
1 tablespoon minced fresh thyme
¼ teaspoon distilled vinegar
Salt

In a sauté pan or skillet, boil the orange juice and chopped shallot over medium-high heat until reduced to a syrupy consistency (about 3 tablespoons of the sauce will remain).

In a bowl with a wooden spoon or in a blender or food processor, cream the butter. Add the orange syrup, thyme, and vinegar and blend until well incorporated. Add salt to taste. Serve a dollop of butter on each piece of fish. Redfish, salmon, and sea basses are recommended. *Serves 6.*

Fennel-Citrus Relish

1 large fennel bulb
½ cup unsalted butter
1 orange
1 lemon
½ pink grapefruit
Salt

Cut the fennel bulb in half lengthwise. Slice the white bulb and 1 inch of the green stems into long, thin slices. In a large sauté pan or skillet, cook the fennel and ¼ cup of the butter over medium heat until the fennel is soft but still crunchy, about 5 minutes.

Peel the citrus fruits, scraping away as much white pith as possible. Break into segments and cut into bite-sized pieces. Add the citrus to the fennel in the pan and warm gently. Stir the remaining ¼ cup of the butter into the fennel mixture, being very careful not to break apart the citrus pieces. Add salt to taste. Serve alongside fish. Recommended: sole, fluke, halibut. *Serves 6.*

Grape-Ginger Glaze

The amount of honey used in this recipe should balance the acid in the grapes. If the grapes are very sweet, you might want to omit the honey.

1 pound red or purple seedless grapes
1 tablespoon red wine vinegar
1 tablespoon honey
1 cup dry red wine
½ cup thinly sliced fresh ginger

Save a few grapes for garnish and place the rest in a large sauté pan or skillet with the vinegar, honey, wine, and ginger. Bring to a boil, reduce heat and simmer for 5 minutes or until most of the liquid is gone.

In a blender or food processor, purée the grape mixture for 1 minute. Force through a fine sieve back into the sauté pan. Return to medium heat and boil the juice down until it forms a syrupy consistency. Brush onto the fish and garnish with the reserved grapes. Serve on shark, yellow-tailed jack, or tuna. *Serves 6.*

Raspberry and Rosemary Vinaigrette

¼ cup raspberry vinegar
1 teaspoon Dijon mustard
1 tablespoon chopped fresh rosemary
1 teaspoon chopped shallot
Dash salt and ground white pepper
24 fresh raspberries
1 cup olive oil

In a blender or food processor, combine the vinegar, mustard, rosemary, shallot, salt, pepper, and most of the raspberries (save a few to use as garnish). Purée until smooth. Then, with the motor running, add the oil slowly. Taste the vinaigrette and, if it lacks sweetness, add a dash of sugar. Serve with swordfish, marlin, tuna, or other oily fish. *Serves 6.*

Brie Cheesecake

*T*his dessert is rich without being heavy. The use of soft-ripening double or triple cream cheese gives cheesecake a whole new personality. The recipe is simple; just be sure to cream the cheese with the sugar before adding the eggs, and scrape the sides and bottom of the bowl several times during the mixing process. Fresh fruit sauce or purée would be especially good with this cake.

10 ounces natural cream cheese
12 ounces skinned Brie cheese, or a mixture
   of Brie and another French triple *crème*
   cheese
1¼ cups sugar
5 eggs

In a blender or food processor, blend the cream cheese, Brie, and ¾ cup of the sugar until smooth. Stop the machine and scrape down the sides once or twice while blending. Beat the eggs lightly; add them and the remaining ½ cup of the sugar to the cheese-sugar mixture. Purée until smooth and liquid.

Pour into a well-buttered 9-inch spring-form pan. Set the pan in a larger container filled with boiling water. The water bath should come halfway up the sides of the spring-form pan.

Place in a preheated 325° oven and bake for 1¼ hours, or until lightly browned and firm to the touch. Remove the cake from the water bath and cool. Invert onto a plate, remove the bottom of the spring-form pan, and smooth out the surface of the cheesecake. Top with a fresh fruit sauce or purée, depending on seasonal availability. *Serves 8 to 10.*

Collectively owned and operated, the Cheese Board is located at the heart of North Berkeley's "gourmet ghetto." Customers are greeted by an inviting wood and glass counter, running the depth of the store, which displays every cheese you could ever imagine, and many more beyond that. Is all this variety confusing? The people behind the counter will be delighted to offer you suggestions and a taste of anything you'd like to try. Your selections will then be cut to your specifications, weighed, wrapped, and packaged in recycled paper bags, an unusual policy even in ecology-minded Berkeley. In addition to the cheeses, the shop offers magnificent home-baked breads, fresh dairy products, and pizza slices for a gourmet lunch on the run.

Compliments of

CHEESE BOARD
BERKELEY

Asiago Bread

Created by Bob Waks, this is a splendid, easy bread, fragrant with onions, cheese, and herbs. It can be made with different cheeses and herbs, but this particular combination is especially successful. Asiago bread makes wonderful toast.

1 package (1 tablespoon) dry yeast
2 cups lukewarm water (105° to 115°)
6 cups unbleached all-purpose flour
2 cups chopped onions
2 teaspoons dried marjoram
2 teaspoons salt
2 cups domestic Asiago cheese, cut in small
   cubes (about 12 ounces)
Sesame seeds

Dissolve the yeast in the water in a large bowl; let sit until foaming, 5 to 15 minutes. Mix all the other ingredients, except the cheese and sesame seeds, into the bowl, adding enough flour to make a medium-stiff dough. Gather the dough into a ball and knead on a lightly floured surface for 10 minutes. Cover with a damp towel and let rise in a warm place for 1 hour or until the dough doubles in size. Incorporate the cheese into the dough.

Divide the dough into 6 strands and braid them into 2 loaves. Brush or spray the loaves with water and sprinkle liberally with sesame seeds. Place immediately in a preheated 400° oven for 10 minutes. Reduce the heat to 350° and bake for 30 to 45 minutes, or until the loaves are well browned and sound hollow when removed from the pans and tapped on the bottom. *Makes 2 loaves.*

Mock Boursin

Herbed Cream Cheese

This cheese is simple to make. The recipe allows you to modify the seasonings if you wish, and it will produce a quantity sufficient to meet your guests' demands. Be sure to use natural cream cheese without emulsifiers, or you won't be able to reproduce the light texture that is essential to this spread. And use only fresh chives and parsley.

1 to 2 garlic cloves
½ cup minced chives
½ cup minced parsley
⅔ pound natural cream cheese, at room
   temperature
⅔ cup baker's cheese
Salt to taste

Crush the garlic, chives, and parsley in a mortar, then blend into the cheese with a wooden spoon. Add salt to taste. *Makes 2 cups.*

In the best tradition of a French three-star restaurant, owner Alice Waters has developed a network of purveyors who supply her restaurant with products ranging from baby lettuces and fresh herbs to the flowers for the arrangements that are a hallmark of Chez Panisse. Waters popularized the concept of a menu that changes daily and uses seasonal ingredients in surprising combinations. The results are exotic and intriguing, and Chez Panisse has developed an international reputation. The restaurant has always been the proving ground for new dishes, as well as the training ground for a corps of chefs, many of whom have gone on to start their own restaurants.

Located in an unassuming, Craftsman-style building, Chez Panisse now has two dining areas: the downstairs, serving one menu each evening, is more formal, while the upstairs is casual and bustling and offers a broader, less-expensive menu.

Compliments of

CHEZ PANISSE
BERKELEY

Grilled Summer Vegetable Pasta

Arrange your meal preparations so that there will be no distractions when grilling the vegetables for this dish, as they scorch easily, particularly the eggplant and onions. Roma, or plum, tomatoes work best for this dish; other tomatoes are too juicy. Consider grilling the vegetables an hour before serving; they will hold up well. If you do grill the vegetables ahead of time and cook the tomato-garlic element of the sauce in advance, the dish can be completed in five minutes.

2 salt-packed anchovies
Virgin olive oil
3 peppers: yellow, green, or red
6 to 8 small Japanese eggplants
Salt and pepper to taste
8 Roma (plum) tomatoes
1 young red onion
1 to 2 garlic cloves
A few basil leaves
Fresh *tagliatelle* pasta for 2 (6 ounces)
Freshly ground black pepper

Fillet and rinse the anchovies. Pound them in a mortar with a little olive oil to make a smooth paste.

Light a mesquite charcoal fire in an open grill. While the charcoal is still flaming, grill the peppers so that the skin is black and blistered all around. Peel and seed the peppers (see Basics), then cut them into wide strips. Cut the unpeeled eggplants in lengthwise slices about ¼ inch thick. Brush the slices with olive oil and season with salt and pepper. Grill them over the hot fire a few minutes on each side so that they are lightly browned. Cut the tomatoes in half and season with salt and pepper. Grill them skin side down until they get a little color and begin to soften. Slice the onion in rings. Brush with olive oil, season, and grill until browned and tender. Mince the garlic. Cut the basil leaves into a chiffonnade.

Combine the anchovy paste, tomato halves, garlic, and a tablespoon of olive oil in a sauté pan or skillet. Cook gently for a few minutes until the tomatoes release their juices and form a sauce. Add the grilled vegetables and continue to simmer a few minutes more.

Cook the pasta in a large amount of boiling salted water about 2 to 3 minutes until *al dente*; drain and add to the vegetables. Season with black pepper and toss the noodles well in the juices. Serve garnished with all the vegetables and the chiffonnade of basil.
Serves 2.

Almond Semifreddo

Elegant and spectacular, this dessert exacts a price in effort. A sponge cake (made to rise only by the air beaten into a mixture of eggs and sugar, into which is folded flour and butter) is baked and soaked in kirsch. Then praline (yes, you make it), chocolate, and whipped cream are folded into a tricky custard, cooked by the heat of a syrup that must be at a specific temperature, to make an ice cream. The cake and ice cream are frozen together, then unmolded and decorated with fine pipings of chocolate. Your guests will be astounded! And so will you, for following the recipe exactly does yield successful results. And there is the advantage that the dessert can, and even should, be made the day ahead. Since this recipe makes two semifreddos, one can be frozen to serve later. Two semifreddos will serve ten to twelve people, making this an excellent dessert for a large party. Finally, match the labor investment with a material one; buy a bottle of imported kirsch. It has the real flavor, and no domestic imitation can match it.

Cake

3 eggs
½ cup sugar
⅔ cup cake flour
⅛ teaspoon salt
2 tablespoons warm melted butter
½ teaspoon vanilla extract

Praline

¼ cup sugar
1 tablespoon water
¼ cup unblanched whole almonds

3 tablespoons kirsch mixed with
3 tablespoons water

Filling

¼ cup sugar
4 tablespoons water
3 egg yolks
1 cup heavy cream
1½ tablespoons kirsch
1 ounce (1 square) finely chopped semisweet
    chocolate
Semisweet chocolate

Make the cake first. Butter a 9-inch-square cake pan, lining the bottom with parchment or waxed paper. Put the eggs and sugar in a stainless-steel mixing bowl. Sift the cake flour onto a piece of waxed paper, then measure it into a bowl, then mix in the salt.

Beat the eggs and sugar together over hot water until they are warm to the touch. Remove the mixture from the heat and beat until it is thick and almost white. The bubbles in the mixture should be very fine, and it should hold a shape for 2 or 3 seconds when the beater is lifted from it.

Put the flour into a sieve and begin to shake a thin layer of flour over the egg mixture. Fold it in, giving the spatula a shake as you bring it up through the flour to break up any lumps that might form. Do not fold the flour in completely. Shake in some more flour and continue in this way until all the flour is almost, but not quite completely, folded in.

Check the butter to be sure it feels slightly warm to the touch, and put the vanilla in it. Dribble some of it very lightly over the top of the batter; don't let it sink through. Fold it carefully with a few strokes and finish adding the rest of the butter in the same way. Be very careful not to overwork the batter or it will deflate. The batter should take about 3 additions altogether.

Pour into the prepared pan and bake in a preheated 350° oven for about 25 minutes, or until the top springs back when it is pressed lightly and the cake is beginning to pull away from the sides of the pan. Cool in the pan 5 minutes; then turn out on a rack to finish cooling.

Make the praline next. Butter a 9-inch pan. Heat the sugar and water in a small, heavy, light-colored saucepan. (It's hard to keep track of the color of cooking sugar in a dark pan.) When the sugar has melted, add the almonds and continue cooking, stirring slightly when necessary, until the sugar has turned a light caramel color. If sugar begins to crystallize on the almonds, stir them around gently until the sugar melts off them. When all the sugar is melted and caramelized, pour it into the buttered pan, making sure the nuts are in a single layer. Cool, turn out, and chop fine by hand.

Line two 9-by-5-inch loaf pans with plastic wrap and cut a piece of the cake to fit the bottom of each. Sprinkle the cake with the kirsch-water mixture.

To make the filling, put the sugar and water into a small saucepan and cook to 230°, or until it spins a 1-inch thread when a spoon is dipped in and pulled out. While that cooks, beat the egg yolks until they hold a shape. When the syrup is ready, pour it into the egg yolks in a thin stream, being careful to beat constantly and to beat where the syrup is hitting the yolks so they don't curdle. Beat over ice until cool and thick enough to hold a shape.

Whip the cream with the kirsch until it is as thick as the egg mixture. Fold them together. (The resulting mixture must be thick enough to hold the praline and chocolate in suspension.)

Fold in the chocolate and the praline and pour into the pans on top of the cake. Cover with plastic wrap and freeze.

To serve, cut in slices about ¾ inch thick. Melt a little chocolate and put through a very fine pastry tube in slanting lines across each slice (or use the tines of a fork). *Serves 10 to 12 (makes 2 semifreddos).*

NOTE: A hazelnut variation can be made by substituting ¼ cup hazelnuts for the almonds. Toast them in a 375° oven for 5 minutes, then cool them and rub off as many of their skins as possible. Proceed, substituting cognac for the kirsch in the recipe above.

Macadamia Nut and Coconut Tart

Exotic ingredients and old-fashioned techniques combine to make an unusually good dessert.

Pastry Shell

½ cup unsalted butter
1 cup unbleached all-purpose flour
1 tablespoon sugar
3 to 4 drops each almond and vanilla extract
1 tablespoon water

½ cup unsweetened shredded coconut
1¼ cups macadamia nuts
6 tablespoons butter
3 tablespoons honey
3 tablespoons heavy cream
3 egg yolks
⅜ cup brown sugar
Vanilla extract to taste

To make the tart shell, cut the butter into bits and let it soften slightly. Mix the flour with the sugar in a bowl. With a pastry cutter or with your fingers, cut the butter into the flour mixture until it resembles very coarse meal. Mix the almond and vanilla extracts with the water and quickly stir into the butter and flour. Gather the dough into a ball and flatten it slightly. Cover it with plastic wrap and chill for at least 1 hour.

Allow the dough to stand at room temperature until it is malleable, then press it into a 9-inch tart ring. (Do not use a black tart pan or the shell will burn when you prebake it.) Cover the shell lightly with plastic wrap and chill for an hour in the freezer.

Bake the tart shell in the lower third of a preheated 375° oven for about 25 minutes, or until it is golden brown. Prick the bottom gently during the baking as it begins to puff. Remove the shell from the oven, cool, and set aside.

Toast the coconut and nuts in the preheated 375° oven until light golden brown, stirring occasionally to toast it evenly—it will take 2 or 3 minutes. Toast the nuts at the same time until lightly browned.

Melt the butter with the honey, stir in the cream, and stir that combination into the egg yolks and sugar, whisking just until thoroughly mixed. When the nuts have cooled enough to handle, chop them coarsely (into ¼-inch to ⅜-inch chunks) and shake them in a strainer to remove the dusty particles.

Add the nuts and coconut to the sugar mixture, stirring to mix, and add a little vanilla to taste. Pour into the prebaked shell and bake in a preheated 375° oven for about 20 minutes or until set. Serve with blood orange or tangerine ice cream or *crème Chantilly*. *Serves 8.*

Compliments of

CHIN SZCHAWN
ALBANY

One of the first Szechwan restaurants in the area, Chin Szchawn helped to introduce local tastebuds to unusual cuisines. The restaurant was recently sold to Wesley Lau, a Burmese, and some of his native recipes have been added to the original menu. A blend of Thai and Indian cuisines, Burmese cooking also shows some Chinese influence. Hidden behind an unprepossessing storefront, the candlelit interior of Chin Szchawn is a contrast to the usual bustle of most Chinese restaurants.

Hot Oil Lamb or Beef

A dish that shows the influence of Burma's neighbor, India. The use of cumin and the way in which the onions, ginger, and garlic are browned and then cooked with the spices before any liquid is added are reminiscent of Bengali cooking. It is important to use enough oil to keep the onions, garlic, and ginger from sticking and scorching during the browning process; they must almost deep-fry, and they must brown thoroughly. The result is that the oil is imbued with flavor, nearly taking the place of the meat and thus indicating the peasant origins of the dish. We found in testing that lamb worked better with these spices than beef. In either case, be sure to cook the meat until it is very tender.

1 pound boneless lamb or beef
½ cup peanut oil
2 large onions, minced
5 garlic cloves, minced
1 teaspoon chopped fresh ginger
  (use 1½ teaspoons for lamb)
1 teaspoon cayenne
5 bay leaves
5 dried whole red peppers
1 teaspoon ground cumin
  (use 1½ teaspoons for lamb)
½ teaspoon salt
1 cup hot water
Handful of cilantro sprigs, cut 2 to 3 inches
  long

Cut the meat into 1-inch cubes. Heat the oil in a wok or heavy skillet and cook the onions, garlic, and ginger until brown. Add the meat, cayenne, bay leaves, peppers, and cumin. Continue cooking until the flavors mix well. Add the salt and water, cover, and cook for 30 minutes over low heat until the meat is tender. Uncover, add cilantro, and cook until the oil and gravy separate. *Serves 4.*

Spicy Fish with Sweet Tamarind, Burmese Style

This is an unusual Burmese dish that is simple to prepare. The key to the dish's flavor is in browning the onions, just as in Hot Oil Lamb or Beef.

1 pound fillet of rockfish, sea bass, or other firm, white-fleshed fish
2 tablespoons tamarind pulp or concentrate
1½ cups hot water
2 medium onions, minced
5 garlic cloves, minced
¼ cup olive oil
1 teaspoon paprika
1 teaspoon red chili powder, or 1 teaspoon dried red pepper flakes
5 bay leaves
2 tablespoons fish sauce
1½ teaspoons sugar
Cilantro sprigs

Cut the fish into finger-sized pieces. Soak the tamarind pulp or concentrate in the water for 10 minutes to soften. While it is soaking, brown the onions and garlic in the olive oil in a large sauté pan or skillet. Add the paprika, chili powder or pepper flakes, and bay leaves. Mix well and add the fish. Continue cooking until the spices are aromatic. Add the tamarind juice, fish sauce, and sugar. Cover and simmer for 15 to 20 minutes, or until the fish is done and the sauce has thickened. Garnish with cilantro to serve. *Serves 2 to 4.*

*T*rained in top restaurants, Christopher Cheung is a good example of a "new" Berkeley chef. He has synthesized a mixed (Asian/Mexican) culinary background to produce wonderfully innovative and eclectic fare. Indeed, his restaurant has become so popular that he has moved from his original cramped quarters to a larger location. He explains his approach: "I combine Chinese frying techniques and fresh Mexican and Thai chilies to create interesting and spicy recipes."

Compliments of

CHRISTOPHER'S CAFE
BERKELEY

Risotto with Smoked Poussin, Saffron, Chanterelles, and Golden Tomatoes

This wonderful risotto calls for some hard-to-find ingredients that are worth the search. If you are unable to find them, substitute your choice of smoked meat for the poussin (chicken or turkey are good choices), good vine-ripened red tomatoes for the golden tomatoes, and a mixture of fresh domestic and dried wild mushrooms for the chanterelles. See the Pasta Shop's recipe, page 123, for preparation technique.

1 smoked poussin, boned and cut into small
    dice (about 10 ounces meat)
6 to 7 cups chicken stock
1 cup golden tomatoes
2 red bell peppers (if using red tomatoes, use
    one red bell pepper and one golden bell
    pepper)
1 cup chanterelle mushrooms, diced
¼ cup light olive oil
1 garlic clove, minced
½ cup dry white wine
Pinch saffron
2 tablespoons minced fresh oregano
1 small yellow onion, minced
2 tablespoons clarified butter
2 tablespoons light olive oil
1 pound Italian Arborio rice
2 bay leaves
½ cup unsalted butter
¾ cup freshly grated Parmesan (or use half
    Parmesan and half Romano)
Salt and pepper
Chopped fresh parsley

Put the bones from the poussin into a large saucepan with the chicken stock and allow it to simmer while you prepare the rest of the ingredients. Roast the tomatoes under a broiler until they are soft and the skins are browned; dice. Roast, peel, and seed the peppers (see Basics); dice.

In a sauté pan or skillet, sauté the chanterelles in the olive oil until lightly browned. Add the tomatoes, peppers, garlic, white wine, saffron, oregano, smoked poussin, and 2 cups of the stock (reserve the remainder of the stock for risotto). Simmer for a few minutes and set the mixture aside.

In a large saucepan, sauté the onion gently in the butter and olive oil until it is soft and translucent, but not colored. Add the rice and cook another few minutes, stirring to coat each grain of rice with oil. Add the bay leaves and 1 cup of simmering stock and stir until it is absorbed. Add another cup of stock and continue in this fashion until the rice is done, but still chewy, keeping the liquid level such that the risotto is creamy. Avoid overcooking. Add the reserved chanterelle-poussin mixture and cook for another few minutes. Remove the bay leaves and stir in the butter and ⅓ cup of the Parmesan cheese. Season with salt and pepper to taste and garnish with remaining Parmesan and chopped parsley.
Serves 6 to 8.

Green Chicken Stew with Lemon Grass, Jalapeños, and Lime

Subtly flavored, just short of scorchingly hot, this stew is an intriguing blend of flavors.

Marinade

1 teaspoon minced fresh ginger
½ teaspoon minced garlic
2 tablespoons peanut oil

1 whole chicken breast, skinned, boned, and
  halved
2½ cups chicken stock
2 lemon grass stalks
1 teaspoon minced fresh ginger
½ teaspoon minced garlic
1 bunch cilantro, roughly chopped
  (about ¼ cup chopped cilantro)
4 green lettuce leaves, roughly chopped
2 *jalapeño* chilies, seeded and roughly
  chopped
1 teaspoon oyster sauce
½ teaspoon sugar
½ teaspoon ground fennel seeds
Peanut oil
Additional chicken stock as needed
Salt

Combine the marinade ingredients and rub into the chicken. Marinate for 30 minutes. Simmer the chicken stock with lemon grass for 30 minutes while the chicken marinates. In a food processor or blender, purée the ginger and garlic, cilantro, lettuce, jalapeños, oyster sauce, sugar, and ground fennel with 1 cup of the chicken stock.

Sauté the marinated chicken breasts in peanut oil until browned on both sides. Remove and cut into chunks. Place the chicken and the puréed mixture into a pot and add the remaining 1½ cups of chicken stock and additional stock if necessary to cover. Simmer 45 minutes, adding more stock if necessary to keep the chicken barely covered. Season to taste with salt. Serve with Thai perfumed rice (see page 26) and lime slices. *Serves 2.*

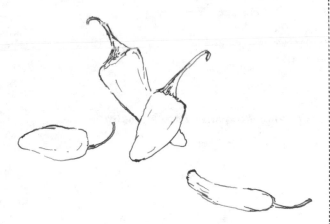

Cold Poached Coho Salmon with Orange Mayonnaise and Watercress Salad

This is a beautiful and impressive dish. Although it is complicated, all the elements can be prepared ahead (but don't dress the watercress) and painlessly assembled at dinnertime. The recipe makes appetizers for six or a light meal for two.

Coho salmon is hatchery-raised in fresh water. It has a light pink flesh and more flavor than hatchery-raised trout.

One ¾- to 1-pound whole coho salmon

Fumet

Bones from filleted salmon
1 carrot, cut into small dice
1 onion, cut into small dice
1 celery stalk, cut into small dice
1 sprig of thyme or a pinch of dried thyme
½ bay leaf
Parsley
1 quart cold water

Orange Mayonnaise (for salmon)

2 eggs
1 cup olive oil
2 tablespoons fresh orange juice
1 teaspoon orange zest

Orange Dressing (for watercress)

2 tablespoons fresh orange juice
¼ cup light olive oil
Salt and pepper to taste

1 bunch young watercress, washed and drained
1 orange, peeled and cut into wedges

Have the fishmonger fillet the salmon or fillet it yourself; in either case, reserve the bones. Combine the *fumet* ingredients in a large shallow pan and simmer for 1 hour. Strain the fumet. Poach the salmon, filleted into 2 sides, in the simmering fumet for about 3 to 5 minutes. (Add boiling water to cover fish if needed.) The fish should be slightly translucent in the center when done. Carefully remove the fish from the fumet with a slotted spatula and refrigerate immediately.

Prepare the orange mayonnaise. Place the eggs in a blender or food processor and purée briefly. With the motor running, slowly add 1 cup olive oil to beaten eggs. Add the orange juice and orange zest. If the mayonnaise is too thick, thin with a little warm water or cream.

To make the dressing for the watercress, combine the orange juice, olive oil, and salt and pepper.

To serve, dress the watercress with the orange dressing and arrange on a chilled glass plate. Remove the salmon from the refrigerator and place in the center of the watercress, top with the orange mayonnaise, and garnish with the orange wedges. *Serves 2.*

Sautéed Marinated Lamb with Thai Peppers, Red Onion, and Hoisin Sauce

Here is a dish to inspire tears and perspiration! It will serve well as an appetizer or first course, but you should follow it with something soothing and allow some time for the palate to return to normal sensitivity.

¼ cup beef stock
1 tablespoon soy sauce
1 tablespoon minced fresh ginger
3 dried Thai chilies, crumbled
1 bunch cilantro, half chopped and half saved for garnish
7 ounces boned lamb from the leg, sliced across the grain into bite-sized pieces (well-aged meat is preferred)
¼ cup peanut oil
4 to 8 dried Thai chilies (optional)
½ red onion, julienned
½ sweet red pepper, julienned
1 large or 2 small *jalapeño* chilies, julienned
1 tablespoon thinly sliced and julienned young fresh ginger
2½ tablespoons hoisin sauce

Combine the stock, soy sauce, ginger, chilies, and 1 teaspoon of the chopped cilantro and marinate the lamb for 2 hours at room temperature. In a heavy skillet or wok, heat the peanut oil until very hot (almost smoking). Add the Thai chilies and cook for 15 seconds, taking care that they do not burn. (If you prefer the dish spicier, break up the chilies.) Combine the onion, red pepper, jalapeño chilies, and ginger and add to the skillet. Sauté a minute or two more and add the lamb with its marinade. Sauté until nearly done, then add the hoisin sauce and chopped cilantro. Cook another half minute or so and serve with hot rice*, garnished with cilantro. *Serves 2.*

*Christopher prefers Thai perfumed rice; see page 26.

Compliments of

COCOLAT
BERKELEY

*T*aught to make truffles by her landlady in France, Alice Medrich brought this Gallic skill back to Berkeley and opened Cocolat in 1976, after she could no longer meet the demand for truffles made in her home kitchen. Chocolate-lovers responded to the shop immediately, delighted to be able to purchase these handmade luxuries and a growing number of classic European chocolate desserts as well. The taste for chocolate in the Bay Area has been elevated to a new level with each new creation. One of the best-kept secrets of Cocolat is that the kitchen also produces several wonderful cakes containing no chocolate whatsoever, created for the rare customer who does not subscribe to the prevailing passion.

Queen of California

This rich, elaborate cake, a variation of Reine de Saba, consists of three separate steps and takes a lighter toll on the cook when prepared a day in advance. The cake profits as well, because the glaze seems to need at least a few hours to set up properly. Make sure the cake is completely cooled before glazing. If not, the glaze will never solidify. Oven temperature is also very important.

Cake

3 tablespoons minced dried apricots
¼ cup brandy
6 ounces (6 squares) semisweet or bittersweet
   baking chocolate, cut into bits
½ cup unsalted butter, cut into pieces
3 large eggs, separated
½ cup plus 3 tablespoons sugar
4 tablespoons all-purpose flour
⅔ cup ground walnuts (about 1 cup before
   grinding)
Pinch of salt
¼ teaspoon cream of tartar

Caramelized Walnuts

10 perfect walnut halves
½ cup sugar
¼ cup water

Chocolate Glaze

6 ounces (6 squares) semisweet or bittersweet
   baking chocolate
½ cup unsalted butter, cut into pieces
1 tablespoon corn syrup

To make the cake: Butter and flour an 8-inch round cake pan or line the bottom with waxed or parchment paper. Put the apricots in a small bowl with the brandy and set aside. Melt the chocolate with the butter in a small bowl placed in a pan of not-quite-simmering water. Stir frequently until smooth and melted. Remove from the heat and set aside.

Whisk the yolks and ½ cup of the sugar together until pale yellow. Whisk in the chocolate mixture, flour, and walnuts. Add the steeped apricots and the brandy. Set aside.

In a clean mixer bowl, beat the egg whites, salt, and cream of tartar at high speed until soft peaks are formed. Continue to beat, gradually adding the remaining 3 tablespoons sugar, until firm and glossy. Fold about one-third of the beaten whites into the chocolate batter to lighten it. Fold in the remaining egg whites quickly but gently. Turn the batter into the prepared pan and bake in a preheated 325° oven for 30 to 40 minutes, or until a toothpick inserted about 1 inch from the edge of the cake shows moist crumbs. The center of the cake will test very moist. Set the cake on a rack to cool.

While the cake is baking, prepare the caramelized walnuts: Skewer each walnut on the end of a wooden skewer. Dissolve the sugar and water in a small saucepan over medium heat. Cover and cook 4 to 5 minutes. Uncover, but do not stir. Wash any sugar crystals from the sides of pan with a wet pastry brush. Continue to cook without stirring until the syrup is a medium-dark amber color. Remove from the heat and quickly dip each skewered walnut in the syrup. Set the dipped skewered nuts on the rim of a cake pan to drip, cool, and harden.

While the cake is cooling, make the glaze: Place the chocolate, butter, and corn syrup in a small saucepan and warm gently in a water bath over low heat. Stir until completely melted and smooth. Remove from the heat.

To glaze the cake, cool the glaze until almost set but still spreadable. Run a knife around the edges of the cake in the pan. A cooled cake will have settled in the center, leaving a higher rim around the edges; press these edges down gently with your fingers to flatten and level the cake. Then unmold the cake upside down onto an 8-inch cardboard circle. Spread the edges of the cake with just enough cooled glaze to smooth out any imperfections, cracks, or ragged places. Be careful to keep crumbs out of the glaze pot. Now gently reheat the remaining glaze in the water bath until it is smooth and pourable but not thin and watery. Strain the glaze through a fine strainer. Place the cake on a turntable or plate and pour all of the glaze onto the center of the cake. Use a clean metal spatula to spread the glaze over the edges of the cake. Use as few strokes as possible. Lift the cake up off the plate or turntable (the stiff cardboard circle makes this possible) and set it on a rack.

Remove each caramelized walnut from its skewer, snip off any caramel tails that may have formed, and place the nuts, evenly spaced, around the top of the glazed cake. Allow the glaze to dry before removing the cake to its final serving platter. *Makes one 8-inch cake.*

John Chalik is a lawyer turned gourmet grocer whose enterprising food complex has played a large part in revitalizing this block of Oakland, just over the Berkeley city limits. His store includes his original cheese shop, a delicatessen featuring a variety of house-made items, a catering service, wines, and gourmet packaged goods, all housed in a series of rooms. This complex is now surrounded by other small, select stores, including a produce market, a bakery, and a fish and meat market, providing residents with a delightful shopping alternative to the giant supermarket across the street.

Compliments of

CURDS AND WHEY
OAKLAND

Apple-Ginger Chutney

*S*picy, hot, and redolent of ginger, this chutney is good with Indian food, but it is also recommended for serving with fresh cream cheese on crackers, with aged Cheddar cheese, or as an accompaniment to simple roasts.

1 pound Pippin apples
1 cup raisins
3 small dried red peppers, chopped
1 tablespoon minced fresh ginger
¼ cup minced crystalized ginger
2 cups packed brown sugar
¾ cup apple cider vinegar
½ teaspoon ground nutmeg
1 teaspoon ground ginger
1 teaspoon cumin seeds
1 medium white onion, chopped
1 tablespoon minced garlic

Core the unpeeled apples and cut into strips (the French-fry blade of a food processor may be used). Mix the apples with all the remaining ingredients in a pot. Bring to a boil, then reduce heat and simmer uncovered, stirring occasionally, until the apples are tender, about 45 minutes. *Makes about 4 cups.*

Broccoli Vinaigrette

*V*ersatility is the best thing about this recipe. It can be a simple, tasty one-vegetable salad, or it can form the basis for an elaborate tray of marinated raw vegetables. Try adding hot slices of boiled potato, green beans, and green onion to the vinaigrette to make a French potato salad. It is also good with asparagus (try adding tarragon or dill) or cauliflower (with capers), and it can be used as a chicken marinade or a vegetable dip if mixed with cream or sour cream. The vinaigrette is also good on hot vegetables.

1 cup peanut oil
¼ cup red wine vinegar
2 tablespoons fresh lemon juice
½ teaspoon freshly ground black pepper
1 tablespoon soy sauce
¼ cup creamy Dijon mustard
5 tablespoons sliced almonds
2½ pounds broccoli

Pour all the ingredients except the almonds and the broccoli into a blender or food processor and process until thick and creamy, 30 to 60 seconds. Toast the almonds in a preheated 325° oven for 5 to 10 minutes.

Cut the broccoli into florets by trimming the stalks off at the point where they begin to be tough; split the broccoli lengthwise into attractive spears. Boil or steam the broccoli for about 5 minutes or until tender but still crunchy. Chill immediately under running cold water or, better yet, in a basin of ice and water. Drain well and toss with dressing and toasted almonds. Serve the broccoli within an hour, because it discolors quickly. *Serves 4.*

Burgundian Walnut Bread

A hearty peasant bread. Whole wheat makes for a stiff dough, and kneading by hand can be heavy going, but it is amusing to watch the chopped walnuts pop out as the dough is stretched (they knead right back in). Because of the single rising, this is a fast bread to make.

Try this bread with aged Cheddar cheese and Apple-Ginger Chutney, page 76, or toasted and served with cheese or jam. It's also good as a sandwich bread.

¼ cup honey
2½ cups lukewarm water (105° to 115°)
2 packages (2 tablespoons) dry yeast
6½ to 7½ cups whole-wheat flour
1½ cups walnuts, chopped
1 tablespoon salt
1 egg, mixed with
1 tablespoon milk

In a large bowl, dissolve the honey in the water and sprinkle the yeast over the liquid. Let sit for 5 to 15 minutes. In another bowl, combine 6½ cups whole-wheat flour with the walnuts and salt.

Stir all but 1 cup of the dry ingredients into the water and yeast mixture and mix with your hands to form a slightly sticky dough. Add more flour if necessary. Knead the dough on a lightly floured surface for 5 minutes. Cut the dough in half. Knead each dough half on a lightly floured surface for 5 minutes. Shape into 2 oval loaves. Make 3 slashes across the top of each loaf and place on greased cookie sheet. Cover with a damp cloth and let rise in a warm place for 45 minutes.

Brush each loaf with the egg-milk mixture and bake in a preheated 350° oven for 35 to 45 minutes, or until the loaves are nicely browned and hollow-sounding when removed from the pans and tapped on the bottom. *Makes 2 loaves.*

Compliments of

FATAPPLE'S
BERKELEY

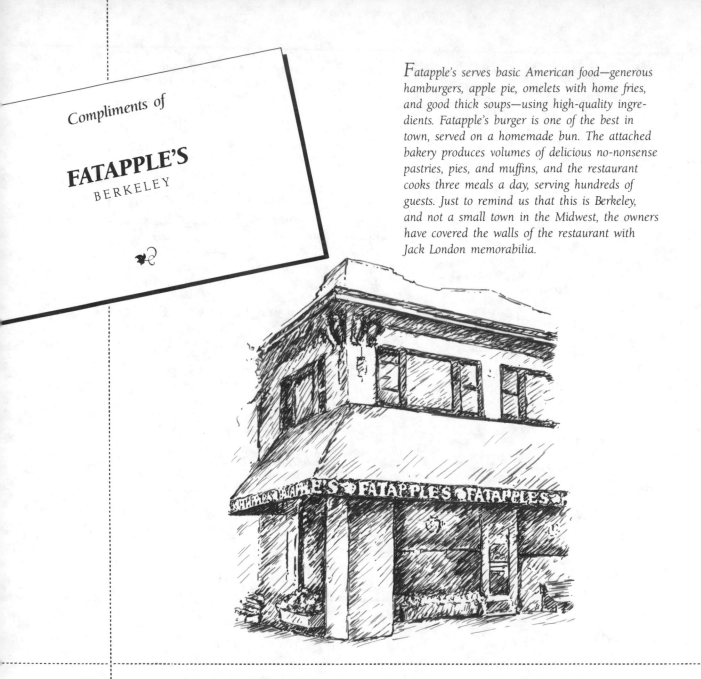

Fatapple's serves basic American food—generous hamburgers, apple pie, omelets with home fries, and good thick soups—using high-quality ingredients. Fatapple's burger is one of the best in town, served on a homemade bun. The attached bakery produces volumes of delicious no-nonsense pastries, pies, and muffins, and the restaurant cooks three meals a day, serving hundreds of guests. Just to remind us that this is Berkeley, and not a small town in the Midwest, the owners have covered the walls of the restaurant with Jack London memorabilia.

Cheese Puffs

For some people in Berkeley, a day that starts without cheese puffs from Fatapple's is a day that should never have started at all. Even if you purchase the puff pastry, this recipe may be tricky to make at home. Be prepared for the possibility that your first batch of cheese puffs may be less than satisfying. Eventually you will achieve success and it will be worth the trouble.

1 pound cream cheese
⅞ cup sugar
1 egg
1½ teaspoons vanilla extract
1½ pounds puff pastry
Powdered sugar

Cream the cheese and sugar together. Add the egg and vanilla and mix until smooth; a blender or food processor is ideal for this. Chill the mixture. Roll out the puff pastry to a thickness of ⅛ inch and cut it into 3-inch squares. Place a heaping teaspoonful of the filling in the center of each square, being careful not to overfill. Pinch the opposite ends of the square together to close, bringing the pinched ends together in the center to form the "puff" shape.

Place the puffs in small muffin tins. Bake in a preheated 375° oven for 50 minutes, or until the bottoms of the puffs are golden brown. Allow the puffs to cool somewhat, then dust with powdered sugar. *Makes about 4 dozen.*

Chocolate Velvet Pie

Stiffly beaten egg whites are folded into a chocolate custard, then the mixture is chilled in a prebaked pie shell and decorated with whipped cream. An optional method of handling the egg whites would be to omit the sugar from the chocolate custard and add it while beating the egg whites, after soft peaks form. This makes it easier to get stiffly beaten egg whites. The sugar can be increased or decreased to suit your sweet tooth.

½ recipe Pie Dough, following, using ¼ cup shortening and ¼ cup butter
1 package (12 ounces) semisweet chocolate pieces
¼ cup milk
¼ cup sugar
⅛ teaspoon salt
4 large eggs, separated
1 teaspoon vanilla extract
1 teaspoon instant coffee (high quality)
Whipped cream (optional)

Prepare the pie dough. Roll out the dough ball as in the recipe, and fit it into a 9-inch pie pan. Line the shell with aluminum foil and weight with uncooked beans or rice. Bake in a preheated 400° oven for 10 to 15 minutes. or until the shell has dried out and holds its shape. Remove the foil and beans or rice, reduce heat to 350°, and bake until brown, 15 to 20 minutes.

continued

Combine the chocolate, milk, sugar, salt, egg yolks, vanilla, and instant coffee in the top of a double boiler. Cook over hot water until the mixture is blended and smooth. Cool slightly. Beat the egg whites until stiff peaks form. Fold the egg whites into the chocolate mixture, blending well. Pour into the cool pie shell. Chill at least 2 or 3 hours. To serve, decorate with a border of whipped cream. *Serves 8.*

Pecan Pie

This is a good, old-fashioned pecan pie, simple to make and sure to please.

½ recipe Pie Dough, following
¾ cup pecan halves
3 large eggs, beaten slightly
¾ cup sugar
¾ cup dark corn syrup
¼ teaspoon salt
1 teaspoon vanilla extract
3 tablespoons cooled melted butter

Prepare one 9-inch uncooked pie shell and refrigerate 30 minutes or overnight. Toast the pecans in a 300° oven for 5 minutes. Mix all the remaining ingredients until well blended. Put the pecans into the pie shell. Pour the filling into the shell on top of the pecans. The pecans should be well covered with filling; they will float to the top while cooking. Bake in a preheated 350° oven for 1 hour, or until the pie is nicely browned and set. *Makes 6 to 8 servings.*

Pie Dough

3 cups all-purpose unbleached flour
¼ teaspoon salt
¾ cup shortening
¼ cup unsalted butter
2 to 4 tablespoons cold water

Combine the flour and salt in a mixing bowl. Cut in the shortening and butter with a pastry blender or 2 knives until the mixture is the consistency of tiny peas. Sprinkle with the cold water, 1 tablespoon at a time, tossing the mixture lightly and stirring with a fork. Add water each time to the driest part of the mixture. Use only enough water to make the dough hold together when pressed gently with a fork. It should not be sticky.

Shape the dough into 2 smooth balls. Wrap in waxed paper and refrigerate at least 30 minutes or until ready to fill and bake pie.

On a lightly floured surface, press 1 dough ball into a flat circle with your hands. Roll it lightly with short strokes from the center in all directions to a ⅛-inch thickness, making a 10-inch to 11-inch circle. Fold the rolled dough in half and ease it loosely into the pie pan with the fold in the center. Unfold and fit into the pan, using care not to stretch the dough. Gently press out any air pockets with your fingertips. Make sure there are no openings for juices to escape. To fill and bake, see individual recipes. *Makes dough for a 9-10-inch double-crust pie.*

*F*ormerly a chef at Chez Panisse, Mark Miller took what is now considered classic Berkeley cuisine and combined it with the hearty cooking of Mexico and the Southwest. The result is a combination of dishes ranging from hamburgers to Louisiana sausages, often featuring the shoe-string potatoes that have come to be associated with the Fourth Street Grill. Located in a building that was designed to house the restaurant, Fourth Street has helped to turn a formerly industrial area into one filled with fashionable boutiques. A small patio has been added to the restaurant to enlarge its seating capacity, but demand always exceeds supply here.

Mark Miller's interest in unusual dishes has produced a series of special dinners with different themes drawn from exotic cuisines. The Berkeley culinary community looks to him for innovative menus, and the restaurant has achieved a national reputation.

Compliments of

FOURTH STREET GRILL

BERKELEY

Roasted Tomato and Chili Soup

A simple soup with clean, clear flavors. If poblano chilies are not available, use any large mild green chili; Italian green chilies will even work in a pinch, but avoid the standard green bell pepper. If you want the soup spicier, include a jalapeño or serrano chili (or two). Queso fresco is a mild white Mexican cheese with a tang unduplicated elsewhere. If you can't get it, substitute Parmesan or dry Monterey jack cheese.

8 large vine-ripened tomatoes, cored
6 large fresh poblano chilies
1 large white onion, cut into thin slices
2 garlic cloves, minced
1 bunch cilantro, tied together
¼ cup virgin olive oil
6 cups rich chicken stock
6 corn tortillas
Peanut oil
¼ cup fresh lime juice
Salt and pepper to taste
1 lime, cut in slices
Grated queso fresco
Cilantro sprigs

Char the tomatoes over an open gas flame, a charcoal grill, or under a broiler until they are soft and the skins are well browned. Do not discard the blackened parts. Chop the tomatoes finely or semi-purée them in a blender or food processor.

Roast, peel, and seed the chilies (see Basics). Cut the chilies into strips. Sauté the onion, garlic, and cilantro in the olive oil over low heat. Add 1 cup of the chicken stock, cover the pan, and let the mixture steam for about 20 minutes. Add the chili strips, tomatoes, and the remainder of the chicken stock. Cook for 10 minutes.

Meanwhile, cut the tortillas into ⅜-inch-wide strips and fry in ¼ inch of peanut oil. Remove from the pan with a slotted spoon and drain on paper towels. Finally, season the soup with lime juice, salt, and pepper. Remove the bunch of cilantro just before serving. Garnish the soup with the strips of fried corn tortillas, a slice of lime, some grated queso fresco, and sprigs of cilantro. *Serves 4 to 6.*

San Remo Pasta
with Roasted Tomatoes
and Black Olives

This is a pasta with pronounced flavors: imported black olives, sun-dried tomatoes, red pepper flakes, and strong olive oil. It is delicious and easy to prepare, but should not be served with foods that it will overwhelm. Roasting the tomatoes gives them a slightly caramelized flavor and removes excess moisture. If the tomatoes are still very wet after roasting, cook them longer in the olive oil before adding the other ingredients. Use plain egg pasta if you can't find red pepper pasta.

2 pounds tomatoes
½ cup fruity virgin olive oil
2 large garlic cloves, or 2 teaspoons minced
  garlic
½ teaspoon dried red pepper flakes
50 imported small black olives, pitted
3 ounces sun-dried tomatoes
Basil leaves
¾ pound fresh red pepper pasta
Freshly grated Parmesan cheese, preferably
  Italian

Roast the tomatoes in a preheated 400° oven for 30 minutes. In a large skillet or sauté pan, heat the olive oil with 3 cups of the roasted tomatoes and bring to a boil. Add the garlic, red pepper flakes, olives, and sun-dried tomatoes, and cook for a few minutes until the garlic has lost its raw taste. Add the basil and turn off the heat.

In a large amount of boiling salted water, cook the pasta for 2 to 3 minutes, or until *al dente.* Remove the pasta from the water, drain, and toss with the sauce, coating the pasta thoroughly. Serve with freshly grated Parmesan. *Serves 2 to 4.*

Compliments of

GERTIE'S
CHESAPEAKE BAY CAFE
BERKELEY

Seafood is the unifying theme for this restaurant, but its variations are infinite. John Shields, formerly a chef at A La Carte, has opened his own restaurant and named it after his grandmother. He has chosen to explore a number of different regional American dishes. As a result, one can sample East Coast and Southern dishes not ordinarily available in Berkeley. Seafood is flown in daily from the East and Gulf coasts and supplemented with fresh local ingredients, an unbeatable combination.

Chicken Liver Mousse Pâté

This decadently rich liver pâté works well as a spread for good bread or crackers and would fit well in a cocktail setting or be good with aperitifs. It is really a little rich to be an integral part of a menu. Be sure to make this a day ahead of time and serve it chilled.

1 small onion, chopped
2 tablespoons chopped shallots
2½ cups (5 sticks) unsalted butter
1 pound chicken livers
½ cup dry Marsala wine
1 tablespoon dried thyme, crumbled
Salt and pepper to taste
¾ cup heavy cream

Sauté the onion and shallots in 1 cup (2 sticks) of the butter until soft. Add the chicken livers and cook for 3 minutes. Then add the Marsala, thyme, salt, and pepper. Continue to cook until the livers are brown but still pink inside and the alcohol is cooked off.

With a slotted spoon, transfer the livers into a blender or a food processor. Mix until very smooth. Cut the remaining butter into small pieces and add to the mixture slowly. When the butter is incorporated, add the cream. The mixture will seem quite liquid.

Pour the mixture into a pâté or standard-sized loaf pan and chill for 24 hours. To unmold, set the pan in a larger pan of hot water, run a knife around the edge of the pâté, and turn the pâté out onto a plate. *Makes 6 cups, or 3 pounds.*

Chocolate Bourbon Pecan Pie

A luscious variation on the pecan pie theme, this is a rich and very sweet conclusion to a meal.

½ recipe Pie Dough, page 80
3 eggs, lightly beaten
1 cup brown sugar
1 cup dark corn syrup
¼ cup flour
3 ounces (3 squares) unsweetened chocolate, broken into pieces
¼ cup bourbon
½ cup unsalted butter, cut into pieces
¼ cup pecan halves

Prepare the pie dough. Roll out the dough ball as in the recipe, and fit it into a 9-inch pie pan. Line the shell with aluminum foil and weight with uncooked beans or rice. Place in a preheated 350° oven until dry but not brown, about 20 minutes.

Cream the eggs and brown sugar together. Add the corn syrup and flour. Melt the chocolate in a double boiler with the bourbon. When completely melted, add the butter. Pour the chocolate mixture into the egg mixture and mix well. Pour this mixture into the pie shell, arrange the pecan halves on top, and bake in a preheated 300° oven for 1 hour and 10 minutes, or until well browned and slightly puffed. *Makes 6 to 8 servings.*

Compliments of

GIOVANNI'S

BERKELEY

Giovanni's is the culmination of the classic immigrant story: owner John Schipani transformed a small shop selling pizza by the slice into this full-scale restaurant serving a broad range of Italian cuisine. Basic hearty Italian fare is available on a daily basis, with a nod to new Italian dishes and ingredients such as Carpaccio and sun-dried tomatoes. Special monthly wine dinners showcase the efforts of local vintners. Giovanni's is a Berkeley institution where you can still find spaghetti and pizza, as well as dishes drawn from the "new" Italian cuisine.

Roasted Garlic and Almond Spread

A simple spread for crackers, bread sticks, or raw vegetables— good with cocktails or aperitifs.

3 tablespoons unblanched almonds
12 garlic cloves, peeled
3 tablespoons peanut oil
8 ounces cream cheese, at room temperature
¼ cup sour cream
1 teaspoon Worcestershire sauce
1 teaspoon Dijon mustard
2 tablespoons chopped fresh parsley
1 teaspoon dried rosemary
2 shallots, chopped
Salt and pepper to taste
⅓ cup heavy cream

Toast the almonds in a preheated 325° oven for 10 minutes; chop. Lower the heat to 275° and bake the garlic in the oil for about 40 minutes, until the cloves are tender but not browned. You may have to cover the garlic to prevent browning. Let the garlic cool, then blend it with the oil in a food processor. Add the cream cheese, sour cream, Worcestershire sauce, and mustard and blend thoroughly. Then add the almonds, parsley, rosemary, shallots, salt, and pepper. Blend again.

Remove the spread from the food processor and place in a mixing bowl. Whip the cream and fold it into the mixture. Pour the spread into a serving bowl, chill for 2 hours, and serve at room temperature. *Makes about 1½ cups.*

Red Pesto

A simple but interesting recipe for pasta, chicken, or fish, which can be adjusted to your taste by the addition of lemon or lime juice, more garlic or less, stronger olive oil, or the addition of herbs or chilies

4 red bell peppers
⅓ cup almonds
⅓ cup pine nuts
5 Roma (plum) tomatoes, peeled and seeded
3 garlic cloves
1 teaspoon salt
1 cup olive oil
⅛ teaspoon cayenne
½ cup heavy cream (optional)
½ cup freshly grated Parmesan cheese (optional)

Roast, peel, and seed the peppers (see Basics). Toast the almonds and pine nuts in a preheated 300° oven for 3 to 10 minutes.

Blend the peppers, toasted nuts, tomatoes, garlic, salt, olive oil, and cayenne thoroughly in a blender or food processor and taste for salt. To serve the sauce with broiled fish or chicken, add the cream. For pasta, add the Parmesan cheese. *Makes 2 cups, or enough for 3 pounds of pasta.*

Compliments of

HUNAN PALACE
ALBANY

Owner-chef Herman Chang worked for seven years at Ghirardelli Square's famous Mandarin Restaurant in San Francisco before opening his own place in Berkeley. A member of an established restaurant family (relatives of his own two other restaurants), Mr. Chang includes several of China's many cuisines in his menu, from the robust spicy cooking of Hunan and Szechwan in the west to the delicate subtleties of Peking cuisine in the north.

Eggplant with Spicy Garlic Sauce

You can lessen the chili content, but the dish won't be the same. It should come and get you. The bland eggplant is a good foil for the forthright flavors of other ingredients.

1 eggplant (approximately 1 pound)
Peanut oil for deep-frying
1 teaspoon sugar
1½ tablespoons rice vinegar
1 tablespoon soy sauce
2 teaspoons dry sherry
1 cup chicken broth
3 tablespoons peanut oil
5 dried red peppers
1½ tablespoons minced garlic
1 teaspoon minced fresh ginger
1 tablespoon cornstarch, diluted in
  2 tablespoons water
1 teaspoon Oriental sesame oil
Chopped green onions

Cut the eggplant into finger-sized slices. Heat the oil to a depth of 1 inch in a sauté pan or skillet until it begins to smoke on the sides. Put one-half of the eggplant in and fry until golden brown and soft (approximately 3 minutes). Remove with a slotted spoon and drain on paper towels, pressing the eggplant to squeeze out excess oil. Cook the remaining eggplant and set all aside.

In a small bowl, mix together the sugar, rice vinegar, soy sauce, sherry, and chicken broth; set aside.

Heat the 3 tablespoons oil in a clean pan. Add the peppers and cook a few seconds; stir to prevent burning. Add the garlic and ginger and cook a few seconds more. Add the liquid mixture and bring to a boil. Add the eggplant and cook about 1 minute, or until the sauce is reduced. Mix in the cornstarch to thicken the sauce. Add the sesame oil. Stir until heated through. Sprinkle with the chopped onion. *Serves 4.*

Bon Bon Chicken

This makes a fairly rich but easily executed first course. The sometimes hard-to-find Szechwan peppercorns can be replaced with ground white pepper, or omitted.

1 whole chicken breast, halved
½ tablespoon sesame seeds
1 tablespoon creamy peanut butter
1 tablespoon sesame seed paste
2 tablespoons distilled vinegar
1 tablespoon soy sauce
½ teaspoon salt
1½ tablespoons sugar
1 tablespoon medium-dry sherry
   (amontillado)
1 tablespoon "hot oil"* (chili oil)
½ teaspoon ground Szechwan peppercorns
1 teaspoon Oriental sesame oil
2 zucchini, cut in fine julienne
1 tablespoon chopped fresh cilantro

Place the chicken in a saucepan, add water to cover, and bring to a simmer; cover and cook until tender, about 5 to 7 minutes. Remove the chicken from the pan with a slotted spoon; cool. Remove the meat from the bones and cut into bite-sized pieces. Set aside.

Toast the sesame seeds 2 to 3 minutes in a preheated 300° oven; set aside. Put the peanut butter and sesame seed paste in a small bowl and soften over boiling water. Add the next 8 ingredients. Mix well.

Arrange the julienned zucchini on a platter, put the shredded chicken on top, and pour the seasoning sauce evenly over all. Sprinkle with the sesame seeds and cilantro. *Serves 4 as a main course, 6 to 8 as an appetizer.*

*"Hot oil" is made by adding 1 tablespoon dried red pepper flakes to 1 cup of very hot peanut oil, allowing it to cool, and then straining the oil. It is sometimes available bottled in Chinese markets.

This restaurant just outside Berkeley's city limits is owned and managed by three women who met while working together as probation officers for Alameda County. They still hold professional positions while they combine their culinary talents. Jackie Karkazis bakes the pastries and the wonderful biscuits that are the stars of the breakfast menu; Sharon Lazaneo does all the dinner cooking; and Kathy Davisson specializes in soups and salads. Inn Kensington was designed to serve the neighborhood, but people now come from all over the Berkeley area to enjoy country-style cooking emphasizing freshness.

Compliments of

INN KENSINGTON
KENSINGTON

Orange, Red Onion, and Avocado Salad with Walnut Oil Dressing

A salad that lends itself to dramatic presentation. The walnut oil dressing ties all the elements together successfully.

Dressing

¼ cup fresh lemon juice
½ teaspoon Dijon mustard
Salt and pepper to taste
¾ cup walnut oil (use 1 cup if a less tart
  dressing is desired)

¾ cup walnuts
3 oranges
2 heads butter lettuce, cored and separated
1 medium red onion, thinly sliced
1 large or 2 small avocados, peeled and
  sliced
24 black olives

To prepare the dressing, combine the lemon juice, mustard, salt, and pepper. Mix well and add the walnut oil.

Toast the walnuts in a preheated 325° oven for 7 minutes. Peel the oranges, removing as much of the bitter white rind as possible; slice into rounds. Toss the lettuce with dressing and distribute the lettuce among 6 plates. Arrange the orange slices, red onion slices, avocado slices, and olives on the lettuce. Sprinkle with the walnuts. Drizzle the dressing on top. *Serves 6.*

Salmon with Fresh Basil Butter

A fine example of one of the area's characteristic treatments of good fresh fish. The composed butter is very clean and simple; don't expect it to make up for inferior fish.

Basil Butter

1 cup (2 sticks) unsalted butter, at room
  temperature
2 bunches basil, leaves only, minced
2 teaspoons Dijon mustard
2 tablespoons fresh lemon juice
Pinch of salt

Eight ¼- to ½-pound salmon fillets

Place all the basil butter ingredients into a blender or food processor and purée until blended. This may take as long as 5 minutes and will result in a smooth green butter.

Bake or broil the salmon fillets for 7 to 10 minutes (450° for baking), depending on thickness (they should be slightly translucent in the center). Top each fillet with about 2 tablespoons of basil butter and serve immediately. *Serves 8.*

The Wangs are Javanese natives who operate this restaurant on a family basis. The menu is devoted to their native Indonesian cuisine. Recently relocated to a large, bright, cleanly designed space, Java serves food unique to the Berkeley area at very reasonable prices.

A blend of Indian, Chinese, and native island cooking, Indonesian cuisine uses peanuts, Indian spices, and a variety of curries. The rysttafel is a good choice for diners unfamiliar with this kind of food. It offers an assortment of both spicy and milder dishes and is available by the single dinner as well as in the usual group portions.

Compliments of

JAVA
ALBANY

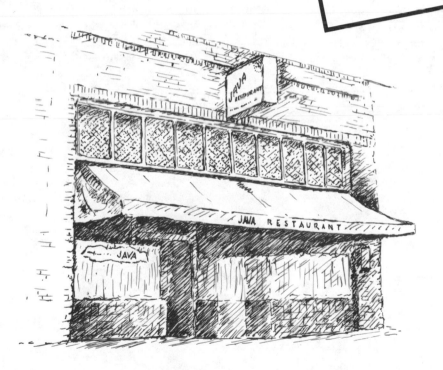

Saté Dagging

Marinated Beef on Skewers

A splendid appetizer or main course in which the marinade doubles as the sauce. It seems to us that the marinade could be put to other uses as well, perhaps on chicken or fish. For use on beef, be sure to use tender, aged steak.

2 garlic cloves
2 *serrano* or *jalapeño* chilies
1-inch piece fresh ginger, chopped
2 medium onions, chopped
1 tablespoon ground coriander
1 teaspoon ground turmeric
2 tablespoons fresh lemon juice
2 tablespoons soy sauce
4 tablespoons vegetable oil
1 cup unsweetened coconut milk
½ cup water
1½ pounds sirloin steak, cut in finger-sized
  pieces
2 bay leaves

Place the garlic, chilies, ginger, onions, coriander, turmeric, lemon juice, and soy sauce in a blender or food processor and purée until smooth. Heat the oil in a large saucepan; when the oil is almost smoking, add the purée and fry for 5 minutes, stirring constantly. There will be much sputtering and splattering, and the frying sauce will give off potent fumes from the chilies. Add the coconut milk and water, reduce heat, and simmer for 20 minutes. Remove from the heat and allow to cool.

Marinate the meat with some of the sauce mixture and the bay leaves for at least 4 hours. Immediately before serving, thread the marinated cubed meat onto skewers and broil, using some of the sauce for basting. Serve the remaining sauce with the saté for dipping. *Serves 4 as a main course, 6 as an appetizer.*

Rendang

Beef-Coconut Curry

Although exotic, this recipe is not difficult, and it gives the cook a chance to learn some new techniques—in this case, frying in coconut milk. Because of its high oil content, coconut milk can be used somewhat like a cooking oil when some of the moisture is heated out of it.

1 large onion, chopped
3 garlic cloves, crushed
1-inch piece fresh ginger, chopped
2 cups unsweetened coconut milk
4 fresh red Fresno chilies, chopped
1 teaspoon ground turmeric
2 teaspoons ground coriander
1 teaspoon ground cumin
½ teaspoon *laos* powder (dried *galangal*)
¼ cup vegetable oil
2 pounds chuck steak, cut into 2-inch cubes
½ teaspoon chopped fresh lemon grass
2 tablespoons tamarind paste
¼ cup boiling water
1 teaspoon brown sugar

Put the onion, garlic, and ginger into a blender with ¼ cup of the coconut milk and blend to a thick paste. Add the chilies, turmeric, coriander, cumin and laos powder. Blend thoroughly until smooth. Set aside.

Heat the oil in large, heavy pot. When it is almost smoking, add the beef cubes and fry, stirring occasionally, until they are browned. Add the coconut mixture and fry for 3 minutes, stirring constantly. Add a spoonful or two of water if the mixture becomes too dry. Stir in the lemon grass; pour in the remaining coconut milk. Bring to a boil, reduce heat, and simmer for 1½ hours, stirring occasionally.

Dissolve the tamarind paste in the boiling water in a bowl, then pour the mixture through a strainer, pressing as much of the pulp through as possible. Add the tamarind liquid and the brown sugar to the meat mixture, blend well, and continue to simmer for another 30 minutes or until the meat is tender. *Serves 4 to 6.*

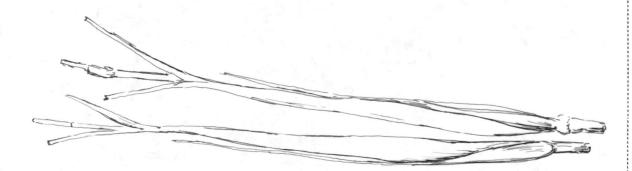

A member of the "second generation" of mesquite-grill restaurants, Mesa presents a simple menu reflecting the market's freshest and most interesting offerings for the day. The addition of fruit wood and grapevines to the mesquite grill adds subtle taste variations to grilled foods. While the name may have a Southwestern connotation, the cuisine is pure California. The restaurant is located in an elegantly remodeled house with an interior done in colors of avocado and peach.

Smoked Trout with Garlic, Lemon, and Chive Cream

In vogue, and rightfully so, smoked trout is most useful as an appetizer or as the main element in a salad. The smoking process firms the flesh of the trout so that, with practice, skinning and boning the fish is easy. The serving instructions call for placing the sauce on the plate and arranging the fish on the sauce, a minor but interesting departure from the ordinary.

½ cup sour cream or *crème fraîche*
¼ cup heavy cream
2 tablespoons fresh lemon juice
2 garlic cloves, minced
6 tablespoons chopped fresh chives
Four 4-ounce smoked trout fillets
2 fresh yellow wax chili peppers, sliced fine
Croutons

In a nonreactive bowl, combine the sour cream or crème fraîche, heavy cream, and lemon juice. Stir until smooth, then add the garlic and 4 tablespoons of the chives. Let the mixture sit for 30 minutes. Slice the trout in a diagonal pattern. Pour the cream sauce onto a shallow serving platter and arrange the trout on top of it. Garnish with the remaining chives and slivers of chilies; serve with croutons. *Serves 4.*

Roast Poussins with Green Plum Chutney

The simply cooked young birds are the foil to a well-spiced chutney. Poussins cook quickly and will dry out if cooked too long.

⅔ cup chicken stock
Six 10- to 12-ounce whole poussins (young chickens)
6 small sheets of aluminum foil or buttered parchment paper
Salt and pepper
Green Plum Chutney, following

Place the chicken stock in the bottom of a small roasting pan. Cover the poussin breasts with aluminum foil or parchment paper to prevent overcooking. Season the poussins with salt and pepper; place them in the roasting pan. Roast in a preheated 375° oven for 20 minutes. Remove from the oven, discard the foil or paper, and split and bone the birds. Serve with a dollop of chutney. *Serves 6.*

Green Plum Chutney

12 pitted green plums, sliced
¼ cup golden raisins
1 medium red onion, chopped
1 small bunch cilantro, chopped
2 *serrano* chilies, sliced
Pinch of ground cloves
Pinch of ground cumin
Pinch of cayenne
Salt and pepper to taste
¼ cup fresh lime juice
½ cup brown sugar
Water as needed

Combine all the ingredients in a medium-sized nonreactive heavy saucepan. Simmer over a low heat until the mixture is fairly thick, about an hour. If the chutney seems too thick or starts to stick, add a little water, or more lime juice if you prefer the mixture to be more tart. Serve at room temperature with roast poussins or other meats. To store, refrigerate in a covered container. *Makes about 1 cup.*

*H*oused in a historical landmark, Metropole is a bastion of French cuisine. The dining rooms of the restaurant provide a faintly medieval European country-inn setting for the three-star training and talents of chef-owner Serge Bled. The menu is devoted to provincial cooking, with an emphasis on seafood and game dishes, some based on recipes dating back to the seventeenth century.

Compliments of

METROPOLE
BERKELEY

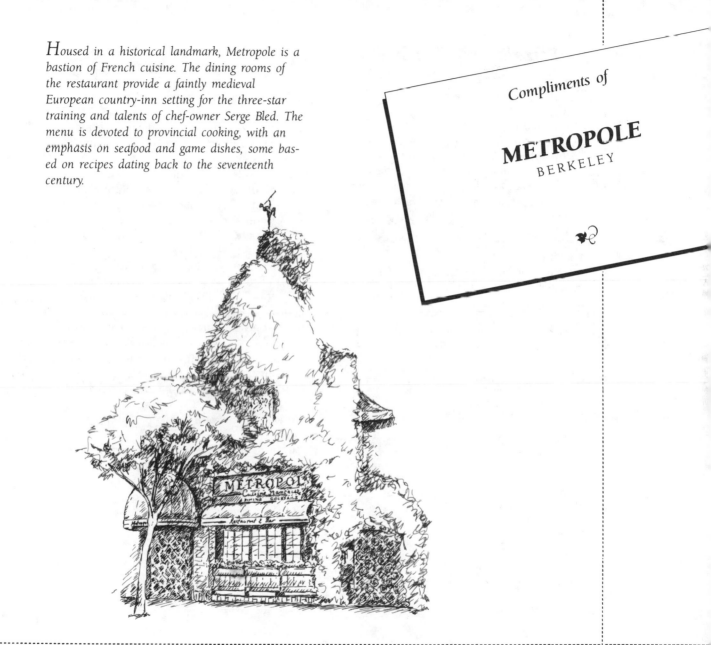

Petrale Sole Boisliveau

Fillet of Sole Stuffed
with Spinach and Endive

An invention of Metropole's chef-owner Serge Bled, this is a dish that has its roots in classic French cooking. As its preparation is elaborate and time-consuming, keep the rest of the dinner simple. A French-style risotto (actually a pilaf made with seafood stock) would be a good accompaniment, while a vegetable course could round out the menu.

1 tablespoon butter
1 tablespoon olive oil
½ bunch spinach
2 heads Belgian endive, leaves separated
Salt and pepper
4 medium-sized fresh petrale fillets, about
  1½ pounds total

Poaching Liquid

1 cup dry white wine
1 teaspoon chopped shallot
1 cup fish stock
4 tablespoons melted butter

Sauce

Reserved poaching liquid
1 cup heavy cream
Pinch of saffron
1 leek, white part only, cut in fine julienne
½ carrot, cut in fine julienne
Salt and ground white pepper

Heat the butter and olive oil in a sauté pan or skillet until foaming and cook the spinach and endive separately, about 15 seconds for the spinach and a minute for the endive, seasoning each with salt and pepper to taste. Let them drain and cool, and then cut the endive crosswise into 3 or 4 pieces. Combine the greens.

Lay the sole "skin" side up (the smoother side) on the work surface and split each fillet in half lengthwise. Flatten them slightly with a cleaver, and season with a little salt and pepper. Place the spinach-endive filling on each fillet and roll up, securing with a toothpick.

To make the poaching liquid, stir the wine, shallot, fish stock, and butter together in a shallow nonreactive pan just large enough to hold the fillets in 1 layer. Place the rolled fillets, seam side down, in the mixture. Bring to a boil, cover the pan, and simmer until the sole is just cooked through, about 10 minutes, depending on the size of the fillets (the flesh should just barely be opaque). Gently remove the fillets with a slotted spoon, drain them, and keep them warm while preparing the sauce.

To make the sauce, over high heat, reduce the poaching liquid by one-half. Add the cream and saffron and reduce further, until thick enough to coat the back of a spoon. Add the julienne of leek and carrot, simmer for 30 seconds, season with salt and pepper to taste, and pour immediately over the fish. *Serves 4.*

Boeuf Gribiche

Beef with Gribiche Sauce

Served with a green salad and a good, hearty rye bread, and the broth from the ribs as a first course, this makes a plentiful meal. For use as an appetizer in a larger menu, use only half the recipe.

4 to 5 pounds fairly lean short ribs of beef
Beef stock to cover ribs

Sauce

1 cup mayonnaise
2 tablespoons cornichons, chopped very fine
1 tablespoon capers, drained
2 tablespoons minced chives (fresh, if possible)
2 tablespoons minced fresh parsley
1 shallot, minced
1 garlic clove, minced
3 hard-cooked eggs, minced
2½ tablespoons French red wine vinegar
1½ cups good vegetable oil
2 or 3 drops Tabasco sauce
1½ teaspoons Dijon mustard
2 tablespoons fresh lemon juice
½ teaspoon honey
3 or 4 drops Worcestershire sauce
Pinch of salt and pepper

Place the short ribs and the stock in a deep, heavy pot, bring to a full boil, then cover, lower the heat and simmer until very tender, 1½ to 3 hours. When cooked, cool, bone the ribs and take off most of the fat. The stock can be served as a first course.

To make the sauce, into the mayonnaise mix the cornichons, capers, chives, parsley, shallot, garlic, and eggs. Combine all the remaining ingredients and add to the mayonnaise mixture, blending well; chill. (The sauce and meat may be kept refrigerated for 4 to 5 days.)

Before serving, slice the meat into long slices, cutting in the direction the bone ran. Put the meat in a saucepan with some of the stock, bring to a boil, cover, and simmer 3 to 5 minutes, or until the meat is heated through. It must be served very, very hot, as the sauce is to be served cold over it. This sauce also goes well with white fish. *Serves 8 to 10.*

Compliments of

NADINE RESTAURANT
BERKELEY

This restaurant is sought out by loyal patrons for its conservative European atmosphere and traditional Continental dinners. Lunches, by contrast, feature a more current California style. Housed in a two-story frame house that was originally the site for the legendary Pot Luck Restaurant, the interior features an enormous central skylight.

Spring Chicken Salad

This makes a gorgeous sight: a fan of endive leaves and snow peas accented by red tomatoes, with white shreds of chicken breast in the center. An easy dish to make, it will accommodate many vegetables other than the ones listed.

½ cup sesame seeds
2 whole chicken breasts, halved, skinned, and
  boned
Salt and pepper
4 shallots, minced
3 garlic cloves, minced
1 tablespoon Dijon mustard
1 egg
¼ cup Oriental sesame oil
1½ cups olive oil or other vegetable oil
½ cup red wine vinegar
Grated zest of 1 orange
½ pound snow peas
2 tomatoes, sliced
2 Belgian endives
2 green onions

Toast the sesame seeds for 2 to 3 minutes in a 300° oven. Remove and increase the oven temperature to 375°. Place the chicken on a buttered pan, sprinkle with salt and pepper, cover with waxed paper, and bake for about 15 minutes or until the breasts are springy to the touch, not mushy or unyielding. Allow the chicken to cool, then slice lengthwise into ½-inch strips.

Blend the shallots, garlic, mustard, and egg in a blender or food processor or with a hand whisk. Slowly add the oils to the mixture while puréeing or whisking. Slowly add the red wine vinegar. Add the orange zest and toasted sesame seeds.

Blanch the snow peas by dipping them in boiling water for 2 minutes; immediately plunge them into cold water. Arrange the snow peas, tomatoes, endives, and green onions on a platter. Place the chicken in a mound in the center. Pour half of the dressing over the arrangement and serve, passing the remainder on the side. *Serves 4.*

Sautéed Sole with Hazelnut-Butter Sauce

The hazelnut-butter sauce can be made an hour before serving (see Basics on beurre blanc*), making the production of this dish very simple indeed. Petrale sole, flounder, or eastern sole is preferred.*

½ cup hazelnuts
¼ cup minced shallots
2 tablespoons minced garlic
1 cup dry white wine
2 tablespoons fresh lemon juice
1 cup (2 sticks) unsalted butter, cut into small
    pieces
2 eggs
¾ cup half and half
2 pounds sole fillets
Flour
1 tablespoon olive oil or other vegetable oil
1 tablespoon butter

Toast the hazelnuts in a 300° oven for 7 minutes. Allow them to cool, then mince. A food processor is ideal for this. Combine the shallots, garlic, wine, and lemon juice in a small nonreactive saucepan and reduce to one-third. Slowly whisk in the butter a bit at a time. Add the hazelnuts and remove the pan to a warm place.

Mix the eggs and half and half together. Dredge the sole in the flour, shake off the excess, and dip the fillets in the egg batter. Heat the oil and butter. When the butter foams but before it browns, add the fish and sauté for 2 to 3 minutes on the first side and 1 to 2 minutes on the second side. Serve immediately, with the sauce on the side or poured over the fish. *Serves 6.*

The most elegant entry into Berkeley's ever-growing group of ethnic restaurants, Nakapan is the offspring of a Bangkok restaurant. After ten years there, owner Orrawan Chaloeicheep came to this country and selected a surprising site for his elegant Thai cuisine: a building with an imaginatively contoured split-level redwood interior. The contrast of exotic foods in a contemporary California setting works surprisingly well; the Bangkok cuisine itself is authentic down to the specially imported covered bowls in which the soup is served. Not all the dishes are as hot as one might expect, and the menu is divided into sections of hot and mild dishes.

Compliments of

NAKAPAN
BERKELEY

Barbecued Chicken with Cabbage Salad

Picnic fare at its best. The cool but spicy cabbage salad balances the chicken to perfection.

9 garlic cloves, minced
Three 1-inch pieces fresh ginger, minced
1½ teaspoons ground black pepper
1½ teaspoons salt
2 teaspoons chopped fresh cilantro
1 tablespoon chopped coriander (cilantro) root or stems
1½ tablespoons soy sauce
1 teaspoon ground caraway
1 whole chicken, cut into quarters
3 tablespoons vegetable oil
Cabbage Salad, following

Mix together the garlic, ginger, pepper, salt, cilantro, coriander root or stems, soy sauce, and caraway. Mix with the chicken pieces. Sprinkle the oil over all. Marinate at least 4 hours or overnight. Cook over charcoal until the juices run clear when the thigh of the chicken is pierced with a knife, about 30 minutes. Serve with cabbage salad. *Serves 4.*

Cabbage Salad

4 cups shredded cabbage
2 cups shredded carrots
5 tablespoons fresh lime juice
1 garlic clove, minced
1 teaspoon sugar
Fish sauce or salt to taste
1 to 2 teaspoons dried red pepper flakes

Mix the cabbage and carrots. Mix the lime juice, garlic, sugar and fish sauce or salt together, and pour over the cabbage and carrots. Sprinkle the red pepper flakes on top. *Serves 4.*

Red Snapper à la Bangkok

This recipe demonstrates the Chinese influences on Thai cooking. The mild and complex sauce blends subtly with the citrus fragrances of the steamed fish. If red snapper is unavailable, any firm, white-fleshed fish may be substituted. The pickled plums are available in Chinese markets.

1 ounce dried black mushrooms
1 cup warm water
2 tablespoons vegetable oil
1 garlic clove, minced
1-inch piece fresh ginger, minced
4 Chinese pickled plums, seeded, and chopped
1 teaspoon sugar
2 tablespoons oyster sauce
¾ teaspoon ground white pepper
1 tablespoon soy sauce
½ cup sliced fresh lemon grass
3 dried lime leaves
2 pounds red snapper fillets
4 green onions, sliced thin

Soak the mushrooms in the warm water for 30 minutes. Drain the mushrooms, reserving the mushroom water. Cut the mushrooms into slices. Heat the oil in a saucepan over medium heat. Sauté the garlic until it is light brown. Add the mushrooms, ginger, plums, sugar, oyster sauce, white pepper, and soy sauce. Simmer for 5 minutes, adding the reserved mushroom water if the sauce becomes too thick or threatens to scorch.

While the sauce simmers, steam the fish: Place half the lemon grass and 1 lime leaf in the bottom of a steamer basket; add the fish and top with the rest of the lemon grass and lime leaves. Steam for about 5 minutes, depending on the thickness of the fish (it should be very slightly translucent in the center). To finish the sauce, add the rest of the mushroom soaking water and the green onions and bring to a boil. If the sauce is still too thick, use water from the steamer to thin it. Serve the sauce over the fish. *Serves 6.*

Green Curry Beef

Another dish from Thailand and, as one might expect, a spicy one. The recipe provides for a milder version.

3½ cups unsweetened coconut milk
Green Curry Paste, following
3 pounds aged top sirloin steak, cut into 1-inch cubes
4 tablespoons fish sauce
½ teaspoon sugar
3 dried lemon leaves
2 cups fresh or frozen green peas
4 green chilies, cut lengthwise into narrow strips (*serrano* or *jalapeño* chilies are hot; for a milder version, use 1 green bell pepper)
2 tablespoons chopped basil
Whole basil leaves

In a saucepan, heat 1 cup of the coconut milk, stirring constantly until it comes to a boil. Lower the heat and continue cooking, stirring occasionally, until the coconut milk thickens and oil bubbles around it. By this time it should be reduced to one quarter of the original amount.

Add the green curry paste and fry for 5 minutes, stirring constantly. The curry paste will smell cooked and the oil will separate from it when it is ready. Add the beef and cook over medium heat, stirring frequently and turning the pieces until they are cooked to your taste, about 3 minutes for medium rare. Add the remaining coconut milk and the fish sauce, sugar, and lemon leaves. Bring to a boil, stirring. Add the peas, green chilies, and basil. Stir briefly. Remove from heat. Serve with steamed rice and decorate with basil leaves. *Serves 6 to 8.*

Green Curry Paste

2 tablespoons peanut oil
10 *serrano* chilies or 2 green bell peppers, cut up
2 tablespoons chopped fresh lemon grass and lemon peel, mixed
1 teaspoon chopped fresh cilantro
1 tablespoon chopped red onion
7 whole white peppercorns
1 teaspoon salt
2 garlic cloves

Heat the oil in a wok or a skillet and stir-fry the remaining ingredients until the chilies are soft. Pound with a mortar until a smooth paste or use a blender or food processor, adding a little water to ease the grinding.

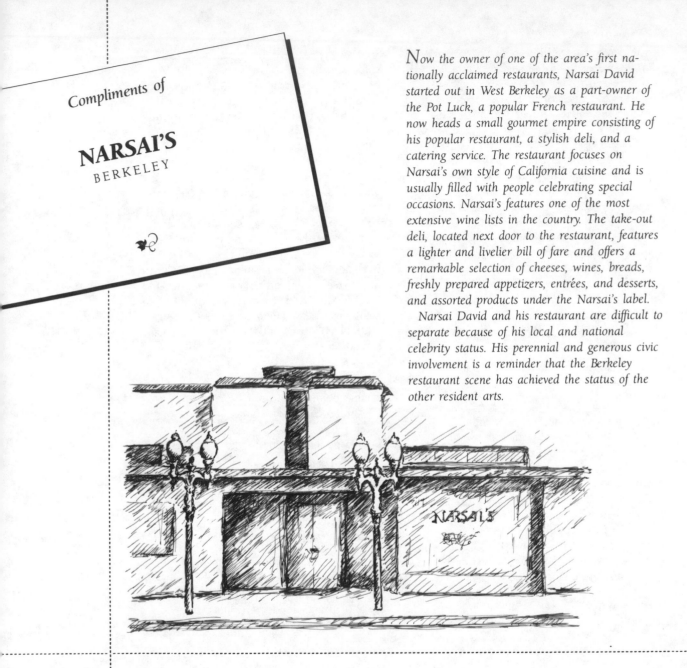

Compliments of

NARSAI'S
BERKELEY

Now the owner of one of the area's first nationally acclaimed restaurants, Narsai David started out in West Berkeley as a part-owner of the Pot Luck, a popular French restaurant. He now heads a small gourmet empire consisting of his popular restaurant, a stylish deli, and a catering service. The restaurant focuses on Narsai's own style of California cuisine and is usually filled with people celebrating special occasions. Narsai's features one of the most extensive wine lists in the country. The take-out deli, located next door to the restaurant, features a lighter and livelier bill of fare and offers a remarkable selection of cheeses, wines, breads, freshly prepared appetizers, entrées, and desserts, and assorted products under the Narsai's label.

Narsai David and his restaurant are difficult to separate because of his local and national celebrity status. His perennial and generous civic involvement is a reminder that the Berkeley restaurant scene has achieved the status of the other resident arts.

Smoked Fish Mousse with Caviar

An easy, sure-fire winner, especially when made with smoked salmon. Rich and expensive, this is just the thing to go with wine or champagne before dinner. Leftovers keep well.

½ pound smoked salmon, sturgeon, black
    cod, or trout
¾ cup (1½ sticks) unsalted butter
Juice of ½ lemon or more, to taste
Few drops of Tabasco
Salmon and/or Beluga caviar
12 to 16 thin slices whole-grain bread
½ cup melted butter

Remove the skin and bones from the fish and cut the fish into 1-inch pieces. Cut the butter into ½-inch slices.

In a blender or food processor, grind the fish very fine. Add the ¾ cup butter, lemon juice, and Tabasco. Purée until smooth. Scrape down and taste. Add more lemon or Tabasco if desired. Turn the mixture into an attractive bowl and decorate the top with caviar, using several types and colors, depending on how lavish you want to be. The fish mixture may also be layered with caviar.

Brush the bread with melted butter and place in a preheated 350° oven on a cookie sheet for 5 minutes or until it begins to color. Serve the fish mousse on the warm toast. Accompany with champagne. *Serves 6 to 8 as an appetizer.*

Lemon Curd Sauce for Fresh Fruit

Essentially a sweet hollandaise sauce, this lemon curd is at its best with raspberries. Any other fresh, tart berry is also good, and the lemon curd would also fit nicely into a genoise with fresh fruit.

You must use a nonreactive bowl (glass or stainless steel) because the lemon juice picks up metallic flavors easily. The sugar may be adjusted to your taste.

4 egg yolks
Zest of 1 lemon, grated
Juice of 2 lemons
½ cup sugar
6 tablespoons unsalted butter, melted
½ cup heavy cream

In a heavy bowl over a hot water bath or in a double boiler, whisk the egg yolks, lemon zest and juice, and sugar. Continue whipping until light and fluffy. Remove immediately from the heat and whisk in the butter a little at a time. Set aside to cool. Whip the cream until firm but slightly soft and fold gently into the cooled lemon curd. *Makes about 1½ cups.*

NOTE: To serve in other recipes calling for lemon curd, omit the whipped cream.

Almond Cake with Raspberry Purée

A simple, rich cake made spectacular by the addition of raspberry purée.

3 eggs, lightly beaten
8 ounces almond paste
¾ cup sugar
½ cup unsalted butter, at room temperature
¼ cup unbleached all-purpose flour
Powdered sugar
Raspberry Purée, following

Cream 1 egg, the almond paste, and the sugar. Beat in the remaining eggs. Add the butter and beat until creamed. Stir in the flour until just mixed in. Do not over-stir. Pour into a buttered and floured 8-inch round cake pan. Bake in a preheated 350° oven for 45 to 50 minutes, or until a knife inserted in the center comes out clean. When cooled, invert onto a platter and dust well with powdered sugar. Serve with raspberry purée. *Makes 8 to 12 servings.*

Raspberry Purée

1 pint fresh raspberries (or one 12-ounce package defrosted frozen raspberries, without additional sugar)
2 tablespoons sugar

Purée the fresh raspberries with the sugar in a blender. if you are using frozen raspberries, purée in a blender without sugar. Press gently through a sieve with the back of a wooden spoon to remove the seeds.

The he ingredients and cooking techniques of the bayous have taken California by storm in the last few years. A recent arrival in this area is the New Orleans Bar and Grill. The menu here is based on the French-Italian-Creole cooking of New Orleans, modified to make the most creative use of fresh California produce and poultry. (Seafood, however, is flown in from Louisiana.) Cayenne, chili, cumin, and lots of garlic and red onion are the favorite seasonings, and entrées are served with homemade Southern-style biscuits or rolls. The recipes included here were all developed by former chef Peter O'Carroll.

Compliments of

NEW ORLEANS BAR AND GRILL

OAKLAND

Deep-fried Marinated Mushrooms

A great cocktail-party dish or appetizer that will keep you at the deep-fat fryer until you run out of mushrooms or patience!

1 cup red wine vinegar
1 cup dry white wine
1 teaspoon dried tarragon
2 tablespoons minced garlic
Salt and pepper to taste
1½ pounds mushrooms
¾ cup cold beer
1 egg
1 cup flour
2 tablespoons fresh lemon juice
1 teaspoon dried oregano
2 to 4 cups vegetable oil

In a deep pot, mix together the vinegar, wine, tarragon, garlic, salt, and pepper. Bring to a boil. Quarter the mushrooms if they are large; otherwise leave them whole. Add them to the marinade and simmer for 4 to 5 minutes. Remove the mushrooms and drain.

While the mushrooms are simmering, prepare the batter in a large bowl by mixing the beer, egg, ¾ cup of the flour, lemon juice, and oregano. Beat together well with a whisk. Use the remaining flour to dust the mushrooms, then dip them into the batter.

Pour 2 inches of vegetable oil into a deep-fat fryer or a heavy pan and heat. Fry the mushrooms in the hot oil until the coating is crisp and golden. Serve hot with lemon wedges or with your favorite béarnaise sauce. *Serves 4 to 6 as an appetizer.*

Eggplant Creole

Don't be put off the by the length of the ingredient list. This dish is easy to prepare, although a bit time-consuming. Preparing the sauce in advance lessens the pressure and improves the flavor, and breading the eggplant ahead of time allows the crumbs to adhere firmly. Frying the eggplant rounds in two skillets is most efficient: Monitor the heat carefully to avoid scorching. Eggplant Creole makes a hearty companion for simple roasts or grilled food.

½ cup butter
½ pound mushrooms, sliced
2 green bell peppers, cut into ½-inch squares
1 large yellow onion, cut into ½-inch dice
2 tablespoons minced garlic
1 tablespoon dried basil
1 tablespoon dried oregano
1 bay leaf
2 tablespoons chili powder
1½ teaspoons cayenne
½ cup molasses
1 cup dry white wine
10 medium tomatoes, peeled, seeded, and diced
3 medium carrots, finely diced
Salt and pepper to taste
1 cup plus 2 tablespoons freshly grated Parmesan cheese
1 cup bread crumbs
1 large, firm eggplant
Flour for dredging
2 eggs, beaten
2 tablespoons butter or vegetable oil
2 tablespoons chopped fresh parsley

In a large sauté pan or skillet, melt the butter over medium heat. Add the mushrooms, peppers, onion, garlic, herbs, and seasonings. Cook for 5 minutes, until the onions and peppers soften slightly. Add the molasses and wine and cook until the alcohol is gone. Add the tomatoes and carrots and bring to a boil. Reduce the heat and simmer for about an hour, or until the sauce is reduced and thickened. Add salt and pepper to taste and set the sauce aside, refrigerating it if it is not to be served within an hour or two.

Mix 1 cup of the Parmesan and the bread crumbs together. Slice the eggplant into ½-inch rounds. Dredge them in flour, then dip them first into the egg and then into the Parmesan-bread crumb mixture. They may be refrigerated until serving time, with a little additional breading between the slices.

To assemble the dish, reheat the sauce if necessary. In a sauté pan or skillet, sauté the eggplant slices in the 2 tablespoons butter or oil. Place the eggplant on heated plates, cover with the sauce, and garnish with a sprinkling of the remaining 2 tablespoons Parmesan cheese and the chopped parsley. Serves 4 to 6.

Norman's recently changed the focus of its menu from French cuisine to seafood and mesquite. The adjustment has been welcomed by the community. A complete change in the interior decor has accompanied the change in cuisine, and the bar remains one of the friendliest places in town to enjoy old Cognacs, Armagnacs, and Scotches, as well as good beer.

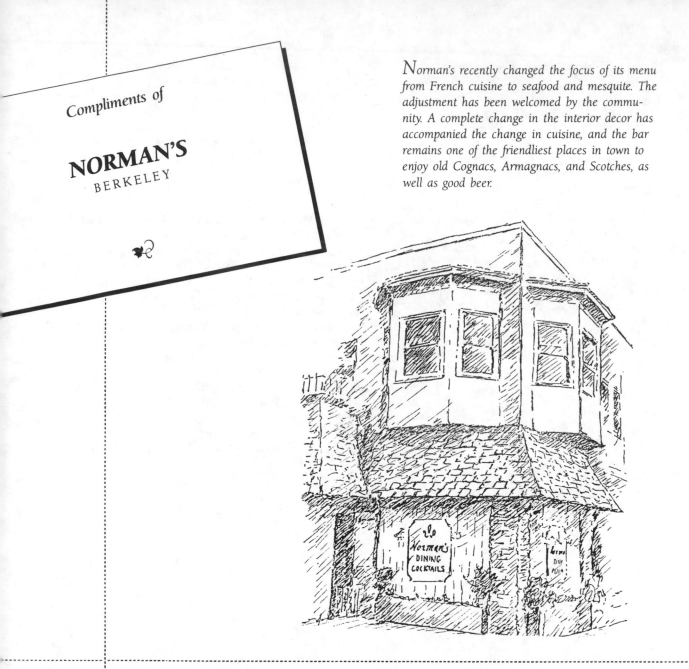

Poached Salmon with Beurre Rosé and Golden Caviar

Use only the best-quality salmon, halibut, or sea bass, and a good-quality dry rosé wine, to make this lavish dish. Beurre rosé is a variation of beurre blanc, page 29.

Beurre Rosé

2 cups dry rosé wine
½ teaspoon minced shallot
¼ cup fresh lemon juice
Pinch of dried herbs of your choice, or
  1 teaspoon minced fresh herbs (fresh
  marjoram or oregano works well)
1 cup (2 sticks) unsalted butter, cut into
  pieces

Court Bouillon

1 small onion
1 small carrot
1 celery stalk
10 whole black peppercorns
1 small lemon, cut in quarters
¼ cup red wine vinegar
About 1 quart cold water

Six 6-ounce salmon fillets
1 ounce golden caviar

To make the *beurre rosé*, in a small, heavy saucepan, reduce the wine, shallot, lemon juice, and dried herbs to ¼ cup. Whisk in the butter bit by bit over low heat. Set the sauce aside and keep it warm. If you are using fresh herbs, they should be added just before serving.

Simmer the court bouillon ingredients in a nonreactive pot for 20 minutes, then strain. Reserve the liquid and discard the vegetables. Bring the court bouillon to a boil in a shallow nonreactive pan, reduce the heat to a simmer, and poach the fish for about 7 minutes. Remove the fillets with a slotted spoon, drain, and serve immediately, topped with the sauce and a small spoonful of caviar. *Serves 6.*

Steamed Sole with Papaya

A hallmark of California cooking is the simple preparation of absolutely fresh ingredients. This dish requires the most impeccable petrale sole, and papaya at the peak of ripeness.

2 pounds petrale sole fillets, split lengthwise
Salt and ground white pepper to taste
6 spinach leaves, or 1 spinach leaf for each
   piece of fish
1 large ripe papaya
1 small garlic clove, minced
1 small slice fresh ginger, minced
Tabasco to taste
Lemon juice to taste
8 to 16 cilantro leaves

Place the fillets "skin" side down (the smoother side). Salt and pepper the fillets and place a spinach leaf on each. Peel and seed the papaya and cut into quarters. Split one quarter lengthwise and cut the resulting eighths into as many pieces as you have fish. Use more papaya if necessary. Place a piece of papaya on each spinach leaf and roll the fillet jelly-roll fashion from the tail end. Secure with a toothpick.

Purée the remaining papaya with the garlic, ginger, Tabasco, and lemon juice in a blender or food processor. Season with salt and pepper to taste.

In a steamer, steam the fish rolls for about 3 minutes, depending on the size of the fillets. Serve with the papaya purée poured over, and garnish with cilantro. *Serves 6.*

*F*ounded in 1977, Omnivore was sold in 1984 by our coauthor, chef Paul Johnston. Based on the principle that people are omnivorous creatures, and the preference of the chef not to confine himself to any single style of cuisine, the restaurant has always lived up to its name. The new owner, Andy Lee, carries on that tradition. Despite the miniscule kitchen, which greets diners as they enter, the food is of consistently high quality. The original recipes and cooking staff remain, and the focus on high-quality ingredients and inventiveness continues.

Compliments of

OMNIVORE
BERKELEY

Mushroom and Pecan Pâté

Since the recipe for this rich and savory vegetarian loaf is quite large, chill the leftover pâté and serve it sliced as an appetizer or in sandwiches with a pungent mustard and cornichons. Another variation is to convert this into a sausage recipe: Roll the pâté mixture in plastic wrap, poach, and serve with the sauce. This dish is an extraordinary treat during wild mushroom season, and was originally designed for chanterelles.

The sauce is related to beurre blanc; *refer to the Basics section for more information.*

6 cups chopped mushrooms (a mixture of domestic, chanterelles, and dried mushrooms)
1 cup hot water
1 onion, minced
½ cup butter
½ teaspoon salt
1 thyme sprig, chopped
8 eggs, lightly beaten
1 cup shredded Swiss cheese (Emmenthaler)
1 cup ground pecans

Sauce

Reserved mushroom-soaking liquid
Reserved mushroom-cooking liquid
3 tablespoons fresh lemon juice
¼ cup dry sherry, Madeira, or dry white wine
1 cup heavy cream
1 cup unsalted butter, chilled

Soak the dried mushrooms in the hot water for 30 minutes. Drain, reserving the soaking liquid for the sauce. Discard any tough stems. In a heavy sauté pan or skillet, cook the onion in the butter over low heat until the onion is soft. Add the mushrooms, salt, and thyme. Cover, raise the heat, and cook for 10 minutes, stirring several times. Remove from the heat, transfer the mushroom mixture to a strainer, and press out as much of the liquid as possible. Reserve the liquid for the sauce. Allow the mushrooms to cool. Mix them with the eggs, cheese, and pecans. Add additional salt to taste. Pack into a buttered 9-by-3-inch loaf pan and cover with foil. Place the loaf pan in a larger pan containing boiling water. The water bath should come halfway up the side of the loaf pan. Bake in a preheated 325° oven for 1 hour, or until the pâté is firm and slightly puffed. Allow to set for 20 minutes.

Meanwhile, prepare the sauce: Place the mushroom liquids, lemon juice, wine, and cream into a heavy, nonreactive pan. Reduce over low heat until syrupy, with only 6 or 7 tablespoons remaining. Cut the cold butter into 8 pieces. Over the low heat, stirring constantly, add 1 piece of butter at a time to the liquid mixture. If the sauce seems too tart, add more butter or cream. Unmold the pâté and serve with the sauce poured over. The pâté may also be served cold. *Serves 8 to 10.*

Green Seafood Soup

A hearty main-course soup meant to take advantage of fresh herbs in season. With the exception of the dried thyme used in the first part of the recipe, dried herbs are not appropriate. The herbs and their proportions are only suggestions. Let availability determine your final choices.

Potato-Fumet Purée

1 medium onion
4 tablespoons butter
2 whole garlic cloves
1 medium potato, diced
1 cup dry white wine
1 thyme sprig, or ½ teaspoon dried thyme
4 cups fish stock

Green Purée

1 bunch spinach
1 cup fish stock
1 bunch sorrel
1 bunch watercress
1 bunch rocket (arugula)
Leaves from 4 oregano sprigs
Leaves from 2 tarragon sprigs
1 bunch fresh chives or green onions

1 cup heavy cream or half and half
4 ounces each rockfish, angler, salmon, halibut
   or sea bass, and sole (totaling 20 ounces),
   cut in finger-sized pieces
Salt and ground black pepper to taste
Drops of lemon juice to taste
Small handful of chopped fresh herbs (chives,
   rocket, parsley, tarragon, etc.)

In a nonreactive saucepan, gently sauté the onion in the butter until it is soft but not colored. Add the garlic and diced potato and stir for a moment. Add the wine and raise the heat, cooking until the alcohol has evaporated. Add the thyme and fish stock. Simmer until the potatoes are tender, about 20 minutes. Remove the herb stem and purée the mixture in a blender or food processor. Set aside.

Roughly chop the spinach, after making sure it is clean and free of grit (it usually takes 3 immersions in water in a large container or sink; the sand will settle to the bottom). Pack the spinach into the bottom of a blender or food processor and begin to purée, adding fish stock as necessary to keep things moving. As the spinach purées, add the other greens, herbs, and onions until they are all incorporated. Set the mixture aside.

Combine the potato-fumet purée and the green purée with the cream and bring to a simmer. Add the rockfish and angler and simmer for 2 or 3 minutes. Add the salmon and halibut or sea bass, simmer for another 2 or 3 minutes, then add the sole, simmering for another 2 to 3 minutes, until all the fish is done. Season with salt, pepper, and lemon juice. Garnish with the chopped herbs and serve immediately. *Serves 4.*

NOTE: This dish can be made with only one or two different kinds of fish, totaling 20 ounces, but a variety of fish will make a better soup.

Suprême de Volaille Parmesan

Boneless Chicken Breasts with Parmesan Cheese

This is an addictive dish; the lemony sauce, crisp cheese coating, and juicy chicken are elementally satisfying. The recipe is simple, with three caveats: Avoid overcooking (a dry chicken breast is a dreadful thing); be sure the butter for the sauce is cold; use the highest heat your stove can produce to cook the sauce.

3 whole chicken breasts, skinned, boned, and halved
2 eggs, beaten
½ cup bread crumbs
½ cup freshly grated Parmesan cheese
2 tablespoons peanut or olive oil

Sauce

¾ cup cold salted butter (1½ sticks)
6 tablespoons fresh lemon juice
Splash of white wine (optional)
Handful of parsley sprigs, chopped

Trim the *suprêmes* of fat and the largest tendons. Combine the eggs and suprêmes in a mixing bowl, making sure the chicken is thoroughly coated. Mix the crumbs and cheese together in a flat, shallow pan. With your left hand, remove 1 chicken breast, place in the breading mixture, and press the crumbs and cheese in well. Transfer the chicken to another pan and sprinkle a bit of breading over. Repeat with each breast, reserving your left hand for the wet egg mixture, keeping the right hand dry. Distribute leftover breading among the breasts. Refrigerate for 1 to 4 hours or overnight.

Heat the oil in a large sauté pan or skillet. A well-seasoned cast-iron skillet works best for this. Avoid stainless steel and ceramic surfaces; the chicken will stick. Cook for about 5 to 7 minutes, then turn and cook another 3 minutes, until the breasts are springy, not mushy to the touch. If they feel quite solid, they are overdone. Remove to heated plates.

To make the sauce, pour the oil out of the chicken cooking pan, or use a small clean saucepan. Cook the butter, lemon juice, and wine over high heat until all the butter is melted and a foamy sauce forms. If the sauce begins to look oily and separated, add a splash of wine. Add the parsley. Pour over the chicken and serve with boiled new potatoes and a simple steamed vegetable. *Serves 6.*

NOTE: The sauce may be varied by the addition of fresh herbs, garlic, capers, chilies, green onions, minced tomatoes, fresh ginger, soy sauce, or lime juice instead of lemon juice, etc.

Fish with Wild Mushroom–Cream Sauce

A rich entrée worthy of the best fish available, especially if wild mushrooms are in season. The basic concept can be adapted to fowl or veal by using the appropriate stock in the sauce and substituting sherry or Madeira for the white wine. We tested the recipe with salmon, to everyone's delight.

2 tablespoons minced shallots
6 tablespoons butter
8 ounces wild mushrooms (chanterelles are especially good), or 8 ounces domestic mushrooms plus 1 ounce dried wild mushrooms (*cèpes, porcini,* or *shiitake*)
1 teaspoon flour
2 cups boiling fish stock
¼ cup dry white wine
1 thyme sprig, or ½ teaspoon dried thyme
2 cups heavy cream
Flour
Six 5- to 6-ounce fish fillets (salmon, sea bass, halibut, or rockfish)
2 tablespoons brandy
Drops of lemon juice
Salt

In a large, heavy saucepan, cook the shallots slowly in 4 tablespoons of the butter. Raise the heat and add the mushrooms, cooking until their water is evaporated and the pan is dry. (Wild mushrooms usually give off large amounts of water. If using dried mushrooms, soak in hot water to cover for 1 hour before cooking.) Sprinkle the flour over the mushrooms in the pan, mix well, and cook for about 3 minutes. Add the boiling stock, wine, and thyme and cook 5 minutes. Add the cream and reduce to the desired consistency.

Lightly flour the fish and sauté it in the remaining 2 tablespoons of butter. Remove the fish to a warm platter. Flame the pan with the brandy. Transfer the sauce to the fish sauté pan, season to taste with lemon juice and salt, and serve the sauce poured over the fish.
Serves 6.

Compliments of

PASTA SHOP
OAKLAND

Owners Marlene Cowan and Shirley Knox had a successful catering business in Berkeley before they opened this high-toned Italian grocery. Much of the pasta consumed in Berkeley restaurants is made here. Spaghetti and ravioli take a back seat to such exotic flavors of pasta as garlic, red pepper, and beet. The store also features a wide variety of olive oils, imported herbs, cheeses, pâtés, salads, sausages, and nightly entrées made on the premises, all reflecting an emphasis on "new" Italian foods.

Mushroom Risotto

A basic risotto *recipe that should stand you in good stead, as it accepts variation with ease. Serve risotto immediately; it becomes gummy if kept hot and does not reheat successfully. The quantity of stock given is approximate. It is important to adjust the liquid when the rice is done, to attain the right creamy consistency.*

4 to 5 cups chicken stock
½ ounce imported Italian or Polish dried
    mushrooms
4 tablespoons butter
½ cup minced onions
1½ cups Italian Arborio or long-grain Carolina
    rice
1 cup heavy cream
Salt and freshly ground white pepper to
    taste
½ cup freshly grated Parmesan cheese
2 to 3 tablespoons minced fresh parsley

In a heavy 3-quart saucepan, combine 2 cups of the chicken stock and the dried mushrooms. Bring to a boil, reduce heat, and simmer very slowly, covered, for 30 minutes. Line a sieve with a kitchen towel or layers of cheesecloth and drain the mushrooms and stock over a bowl; when cool, mince the mushrooms. Reserve the mushroom liquid.

In the same saucepan, melt the butter. Add the minced onions and cook them for 2 to 3 minutes, or until soft but not browned. Add the rice and stir for a minute or two to coat it well with the butter. Add 1 cup of stock, bring it to a boil, then reduce the heat and simmer the rice, stirring, until all stock has been ab-sorbed. Continue to add stock, 1 cup at a time, including the stock used to cook the mushrooms, cooking and stirring the rice until all the stock has been absorbed and the rice is tender but still slightly chewy.

Add the heavy cream and the reserved minced mushrooms and continue cooking until all the cream has been absorbed. Season with salt and pepper, add the Parmesan, garnish with parsley, and serve immediately. *Serves 4 to 6.*

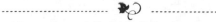

Pasta with Golden Caviar

Caviar makes a pretty plate and an elegant opening course for a special meal. The fresh tomato pasta contrasts nicely with the white sauce. If you are unable to find tomato pasta, make it by adding tomato paste to your favorite pasta recipe, or use spinach pasta for a variation.

1½ cups heavy cream
1 pound fresh tomato pasta
1½ tablespoons chopped fresh chives (green
    onions can be substituted)
Freshly ground coarse black pepper
1 teaspoon fresh lemon juice
2 tablespoons (or more) golden caviar

Have all the ingredients ready. In a small, heavy saucepan, reduce the cream to 1 cup or until it coats a spoon. Cook the pasta in a large amount of boiling salted water for 1 to 3 minutes or until *al dente.* Drain; cover with the reduced cream. Toss in the chives, pepper, lemon juice, and mix well. Garnish with 1 teaspoon caviar per serving (at least!). *Serves 4 to 6.*

Compliments of

PICANTE TAQUERIA & CANTINA

BERKELEY

A welcome entry in the arena of ethnic foods, Picante is a taquería in the true Mexican style. Their fast food with soul is a far cry from the standard freeway taco. The food is similar to what you might purchase from a street vendor in Mexico, for example, marinated broiled meat in a soft corn tortilla with a freshly made salsa. The room is styled after a Western saloon, and the atmosphere is conducive to a family meal or an evening of drinking beer and listening to the weekend jazz band.

Pollo Colorado

Chicken in Red Sauce

This dish is spicy, easy to prepare, and eminently satisfying.

One 3-pound chicken
4 to 5 large dried *ancho* or *pasilla* chilies
2 small red dried chilies
3 garlic cloves
1 tablespoon ground cumin
1 tablespoon dried oregano (optional)
Pinch ground cloves
3½ cups reserved chicken broth
3 tablespoons oil
2 tablespoons flour
Salt
Salsa Cruda, following

Place the chicken in a stockpot with cold water to cover. Boil gently, uncovered, for 1 hour, let the chicken cool in the broth. Reserve the broth and skim the fat. Skin, bone, and shred the chicken into small pieces.

Toast the dried chilies on a hot griddle or in a skillet to soften. Remove the seeds and stems, wearing gloves to prevent skin irritation. (If the dried chilies are not fairly fresh, they may be boiled at this point to soften them further.)

Place the chilies, garlic, cumin, oregano, and cloves in a blender or food processor with some of the chicken broth. Blend the mixture until puréed and add the remaining chicken broth to the purée.

Heat the oil in a large saucepan, add the flour, and cook until it bubbles. Add the chili-broth mixture slowly and cook until it thickens, stirring constantly. Add the shredded chicken meat, heat thoroughly, and serve with rice, beans, sour cream, corn tortillas, and Salsa Cruda, following. Warm the tortillas on a grill or by wrapping in foil in a hot oven. *Serves 4 to 6.*

Salsa Cruda

2 to 3 large tomatoes, chopped
½ onion, chopped
1 garlic clove, chopped (optional)
½ bunch cilantro, chopped
Salt to taste

Mix all the ingredients together well. Serve the sauce the day it is made. *Makes 1 to 1½ cups.*

Salsa Verde

Green Chili Sauce

*P*icante *recommends serving this slightly tart and piquant sauce with red meat dishes, and, while we don't disagree, we found it was also good on broiled seafood.*

8 fresh *tomatillos*
3 fresh Anaheim chilies
2 *serrano* chilies
1 small onion, chopped
Several sprigs of cilantro, chopped
Garlic (optional)
Salt (optional)
¼ cup water

Peel the papery husks from the tomatillos. In a hot skillet or on a grill, toast the husked tomatillos and chilies for about 10 minutes, or until softened, turning frequently. Remove any stems from the chilies. (Seed the chilies if a less spicy sauce is desired.)

Place the tomatillos, chilies, and all the remaining ingredients in a blender or food processor and purée. *Makes about 2 cups.*

This is what happened to Chicken Little after the sky fell. Chicken sausages, mousses of poultry livers, and unusual duck and chicken salads and entrées have made this a landmark in the Berkeley deli business. Poulet reinterpreted the idea of carry-out food, providing people with fresh and imaginative dishes—not only chicken—that achieved the highest culinary standards. The founding team of Marilyn Rinzler and Bruce Aidells took chicken places most of us have never dreamed of, jolting the Colonel back to the dark ages of cookery. Also an original seat of garlic cuisine, this small shop has since doubled in size, adding eating space and a flourishing catering business. The decor is pure chicken whimsy.

Having contributed many of their chicken recipes to other books, Poulet here shows its versatility with recipes featuring eggplant, fish, and other foods.

Compliments of

POULET
BERKELEY

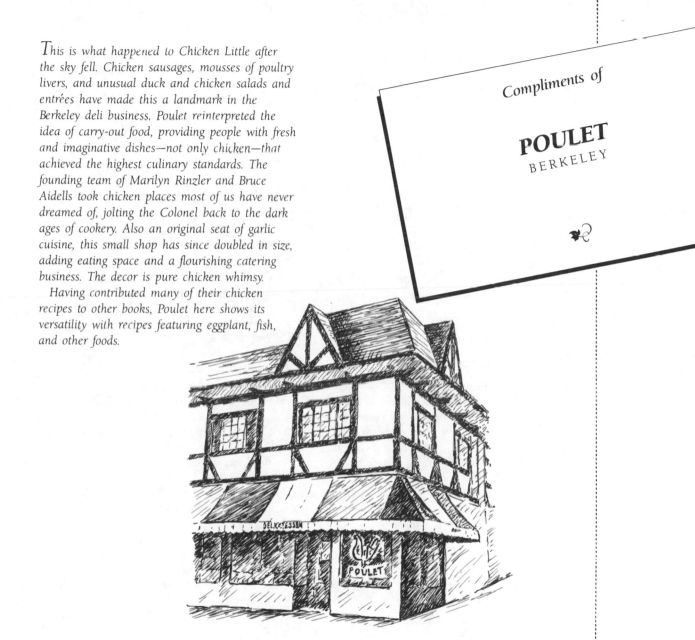

Duck Liver Mousse

A simple recipe, and very good. The addition of apple is a nice touch.

½ apple, peeled and thinly sliced
1 large onion, coarsely chopped
2 cups (4 sticks) unsalted butter, at room temperature
2 pounds fresh duck livers
¼ cup dry sherry
¼ cup brandy
¼ cup heavy cream
Salt and pepper
Chopped fresh parsley or chopped toasted almonds

In a sauté pan or skillet, cook the apple and onion in 2 tablespoons of the butter until they are translucent and golden. Remove this mixture from the pan with a slotted spoon and place in a blender or food processor. Sauté the livers in the same pan for about 5 minutes, until it is browned outside but still pink inside (add more butter if necessary). Remove the livers with a slotted spoon and place in a blender or food processor with the apple-onion mixture. Deglaze the pan with the sherry.

Pour the pan drippings into the blender or food processor, add the brandy, cream, and remaining butter, and purée for 1 to 3 minutes, or until smooth. Add salt and pepper to taste. Pour into a mold and refrigerate for 5 hours. Unmold and garnish with chopped parsley or chopped toasted almonds. Serve with crackers or sliced baguettes. *Makes about 4 pounds.*

Spicy Eggplant

Good buffet or picnic fare, this dish improves over the course of a day or two. The chili content is adjustable. Don't overcook the eggplant, or it will fall apart by the time the dish is ready to serve. Chinese peppercorns, black bean sauce, and fermented black beans are all found in Chinese markets.

½ teaspoon Chinese peppercorns
2 tablespoons chopped fresh ginger
2 tablespoons minced garlic
½ teaspoon dried red pepper flakes
½ cup black bean sauce (if the bean sauce has red chilies, omit the pepper flakes)
2 tablespoons fermented black beans
¼ cup peanut oil
¼ cup soy sauce
2 tablespoons water
2 eggplants
Peanut oil
2 tablespons chopped cilantro
2 tablespoons chopped green onions

Roast the Chinese peppercorns in a 450° oven for 2 minutes or toast lightly in a sauté pan or skillet until they smoke a little. Grind them in a mortar. Purée the peppercorns, ginger, garlic, red pepper, bean sauce, and black beans in a blender or food processor. Add the ¼ cup peanut oil in a stream, then add the soy sauce and water.

Slice the eggplants ¾ inch thick lengthwise. Brush very lightly with oil, place on cookie sheets, and bake in a preheated 450° oven for 10 minutes, or until golden brown. Do not overcook. Cut the eggplant into 2-inch-square

pieces and place in a serving dish in 1 layer.
Spread the eggplant with the sauce and
sprinkle with chopped cilantro and green
onions; repeat the layering 4 or 5 times.
Refrigerate and serve cold. *Serves 4 to 6.*

Seafood-stuffed Summer Squash with Cilantro Sauce

This dish may seem a touch on the bizarre side, but it works beautifully. Use pattypan or cymling summer squash, or try a new variety called scaloppine squash.

12 pattypan or cymling squash
12 ounces angler fillet or other firm-fleshed
   white fish
¼ cup olive oil
Cilantro Sauce, following
¼ cup freshly grated Parmesan

Scoop out the inside of the squash to make
room for the fish. Steam the hollowed-out
squash for 3 minutes, then plunge them into
cold water and drain. Sauté the fish in a sauté
pan or skillet in very hot (smoking) olive oil
until almost opaque in the center; remove
from the pan and let cool. Fill each squash
with a piece of the fish. Top with a little
cilantro sauce and grated Parmesan cheese
and brown under the broiler or in a very hot
preheated oven (550°). Heat the remaining
sauce and serve alongside the stuffed squash.
Serves 6 as an appetizer.

Cilantro Sauce

2 bunches cilantro
1 bunch green onions
½ bunch parsley
¼ cup chopped garlic
⅓ cup fresh lemon juice
⅓ cup olive oil
½ cup heavy cream
Salt and pepper

Put the cilantro, onions, parsley, garlic, and
lemon juice into a blender or food processor
and blend into a paste. Add olive oil as
necessary to keep things moving. Add the rest
of the oil in a thin stream, then add the
cream and season to taste with salt and
pepper. *Makes about 1½ cups.*

Compliments of

RAMONA'S
BERKELEY

Ramona's features a Tuesday night garlic dinner and offers California cuisine in combination with such standbys as good, filling burgers and deep-dish pizza. The menu is suited to the entire family, a welcome and uncommon approach in Berkeley. Owner Bob Kelso began his career in Berkeley as a waiter, then started a thriving bagel shop, and now heads a small food empire including, in addition to Ramona's and Brothers' Bagels, a catering service, a European bakery, and a croissant cafe.

Seafood Linguine with Cream and Pistachios

Created by former chef David Sperberg, this is a dish with lovely colors, especially if you can buy or make fresh herb pasta. It is nicer with a narrow noodle, as broad pasta tends to cover up the colorful peppers.

1 tablespoon chopped pistachio nuts
2 tablespoons unsalted butter
¼ red bell pepper, diced
½ teaspoon minced garlic
8 ounces fresh boneless salmon, diced
1 cup heavy cream
1 teaspoon grated lemon zest
Pinch of salt
Pinch of ground white pepper
4 ounces fresh herb linguine
2 tablespoons freshly grated Parmesan cheese

Toast the pistachios for 5 minutes in a preheated 300° oven. Set aside. Start a large pot of lightly salted water boiling for the pasta. Melt the butter in a sauté pan or skillet; do not let it brown. Add the red pepper and garlic and sauté for 1 minute over medium heat. Add the salmon and sauté for 1 minute; add the cream, lemon zest, salt, and pepper and reduce to the desired consistency. When the sauce is done, cook the pasta until *al dente*, 30 seconds to 1 minute. Drain well and toss with the sauce. Sprinkle with the pistachio nuts and Parmesan cheese. *Serves 2.*

Linguine with Chicken and Goat Cheese

Serve this rich pasta as a main course, or halve the portions if you wish to use it as an appetizer.

2 tablespoons chopped walnuts
2 tablespoons unsalted butter
5 ounces boneless chicken breast, cut into
   1-inch dice
½ cup sliced mushrooms
½ cup dry white wine
1 teaspoon minced fresh tarragon,
   or ½ teaspoon dried tarragon
1 cup heavy cream
2 ounces crumbled goat cheese
1 tablespoon fresh lemon juice
Salt and pepper
4 ounces fresh spinach pasta
1 tablespoon minced fresh parsley

Toast the walnuts for 10 minutes in a 300° oven. Start a large pot of water boiling for the pasta. In a sauté pan or skillet, melt the butter and quickly brown the chicken. Remove it from the pan with a slotted spoon and sauté the mushrooms. Add the white wine and tarragon. Cook until the alcohol smell is gone, then add the cream and chicken and reduce by one-third. Add the goat cheese and melt it into the sauce over low heat. Add the lemon juice and salt and pepper to taste. Cook the pasta until *al dente,* about 1 minute, drain well, and toss with the sauce. Garnish with the toasted walnuts and parsley. *Serves 2.*

Compliments of

RIERA'S
BERKELEY

Local radio personality and restaurant critic Russ Riera turned to Berkeley when he decided to open his own restaurant, responding to the absence of Northern Italian cuisine in this otherwise cuisine-rich city. He has transformed a cinder-block storefront with urban landscaping: bright flower boxes adorn the front wall, and the main dining room features a glass wall looking out onto an illuminated garden. Chef Louis Pasco's Northern Italian cooking fills the menu with seafood soups and fresh pasta, which, like all the bread, is made on the premises. Veal, prepared in a number of ways, is a specialty here.

Riera's is one of Berkeley's few small Italian restaurants, and it is a good choice when the urge for veal parmigiana or piccata hits.

Poached Fish
with Piccata Sauce

This piccata *sauce is a variant of* beurre blanc, *a member of the hot butter sauce family. (For more information on this group of sauces, see* Basics). *The sauce and the poaching technique work well with other fish. Halibut, rockfish, tuna, and shark are particularly good with piccata sauce. Of course, the cooking time must be adjusted to the fish being used.*

Poaching Liquid

3 carrots, cut into chunks
4 celery stalks, cut into chunks
2 large onions, chopped
4 cloves
12 peppercorns
1 to 2 bay leaves
½ bunch thyme (about 12 sprigs)
6 parsley sprigs
1½ to 2 quarts cold water
2 cups dry white wine
Juice of 2 lemons

Four 8-ounce whole trout or coho salmon

Piccata Sauce

6 tablespoons white wine vinegar
2 tablespoons minced shallots
1 cup reserved poaching liquid
6 tablespoons unsalted butter
2 tablespoons capers, drained
Salt and pepper

Combine the vegetables, spices, and herbs with the cold water in a large saucepan. Simmer for 20 minutes. Strain the liquid and place it in a 9-by-13-by-3-inch pan. Add the wine and lemon juice. Remove 1 cup of the poaching liquid and set it aside to make the sauce. Bring the remaining liquid to a boil, reduce heat, and add the fish. Let barely simmer for 10 minutes; with a spatula, carefully remove the fish to plates.

To make the sauce, place the vinegar and shallots in a small nonreactive saucepan. Add the reserved cup of poaching liquid. Boil down slowly, stirring to prevent any caramelizing along the insides of the pan, until only a tablespoonful or so of liquid remains. Over medium-low heat lightly whisk in the butter, half a tablespoon at a time, until a creamy, frothy sauce is formed. Add the capers and salt and pepper to taste, and pour over the fish. *Serves 4.*

NOTE: You can make the poaching liquid and the sauce ahead of time. Keep the sauce on a warm spot on the stove.

Wild Mushroom Lasagne

Good party or buffet fare, this rich lasagne is best prepared ahead of time and baked as needed.

2 ounces dried mushrooms (*porcini, cèpes, shiitakes*)
1½ cups hot water

Bechamel Sauce

3 cups milk
1 cup reserved mushroom-soaking liquid
4 tablespoons butter
½ cup flour
salt and pepper
Freshly grated nutmeg
Fresh lemon juice

1 pound fresh button mushrooms
1 pound fresh chanterelles (available fall and winter)
1 cup (2 sticks) butter, or 1 cup olive oil
Salt and pepper
Juice of 1 lemon
2 cups freshly grated Parmesan cheese
1½ cups feta cheese
1½ cups goat cheese
1 bunch thyme, chopped
1 bunch chives, chopped

2½ to 3 pounds fresh lasagne, or 1½ to 2 pounds dried lasagne

Soak the dried mushrooms in hot water to cover until they are soft. Remove the mushrooms and slice them, discarding any tough stems. Strain the soaking liquid and reserve for the bechamel sauce.

Prepare the bechamel sauce by combining the milk and mushroom-soaking liquid and bringing them to a simmer. Keep hot. In a heavy, nonreactive saucepan, melt the butter and add the flour. Let them foam together and cook for 2 to 3 minutes. Add the hot liquid all at once, beat well with a whisk, reduce the heat, and simmer the sauce for 20 to 30 minutes, until the raw taste of the flour is gone. Season the sauce with salt, pepper, nutmeg, and lemon juice to taste. Set the sauce aside, keeping it warm. In a large sauté pan or skillet, sauté all the mushrooms in the butter or olive oil until browned, including those you soaked earlier. Do this in small batches so that the mushrooms do not boil in their own liquid. Season them with salt and pepper and the juice of the lemon. Crumble the cheeses together. Mix the thyme and chives together.

Place the lasagne in a large amount of gently boiling salted water. Do not allow it to cook completely; it will finish in the oven. As you remove the pasta, chill it in cold water, then drain and toss with a little olive oil.

To assemble the lasagne, oil a 9-by-12-inch baking pan. Cover with a single layer of cooked pasta. Spread with a thin layer of bechamel sauce. Sprinkle with one-quarter of the Parmesan, followed by one-third of the mushrooms, one-third of the feta and goat cheeses, and one-third of the herbs. Repeat this process twice. Top with the last of the bechamel sauce and the remainder of the Parmesan. Bake in a preheated 400° oven for 30 minutes, or until golden brown and well heated. *Serves 8.*

Italian Wheat Bread

A very successful recipe that yields two loaves of flavorful, crusty, fine-grained bread. The key to the chewy crust of this bread is to bake the rounds on an open baking sheet; don't use bread pans.

½ cup lukewarm water (105° to 115°)
1 package (1 tablespoon) dry yeast
2 tablespoons honey
1 to 2 cups unbleached all-purpose flour
3 cups whole-wheat flour
1 cup semolina flour
2 teaspoons salt
2 cups hot water

Mix the lukewarm water with the yeast and honey. Sift the flours and the salt together, using only 1 cup of white flour. Add the water-yeast mixture to the flour, then mix in the hot water. Knead for 5 to 10 minutes by hand or 2 to 3 minutes with the dough hook of a mixer. If the mixture seems too soft, gradually add the remaining white flour. The final density should permit a well-formed ball of dough to just hold its shape or to very slowly spread a bit.

Place the dough in a large, lightly oiled bowl and cover with a damp cloth. Let the dough rise for 1 hour or so in a warm place until doubled in bulk. Knead again briefly and form the bread into 2 equal loaves. Place these loaves on a greased baking sheet. Let the loaves rise for another hour, or until doubled in bulk again. Bake in a preheated 400° oven for 15 minutes, then lower the heat to 350° for 25 minutes or until golden brown (this may take up to 40 minutes). The bread is ready when the loaves sound hollow when tapped on the bottom. *Makes 2 loaves.*

Smells of garlic, basil, and tomatoes envelop passersby on both sides of University Avenue, where the owners opened Caffè Venezia, then followed it a few years later with Ristorante Venezia across the street. In both restaurants, trompe l'oeil murals transport you to Venice. Diners may choose to rub elbows with other pasta eaters at the informal cafe, seated under lines of clothes hung from windows and balconies far above their heads, or they may eat the Italian version of nouvelle cuisine *at the more formal ristorante. A unique feature of Ristorante Venezia is live opera recitals on Tuesday nights.*

Pasta alla Putanesca

Pasta with Piquant Tomato Sauce

This robust pasta is a great way to start a meal, or it can serve as a meal by itself. Freshly grated Reggiano is excellent with this recipe. The heat of this dish can be adjusted to taste.

⅓ cup olive oil
9 anchovies
8 whole garlic cloves
¼ teaspoon dried red pepper flakes
4 medium ripe tomatoes, chopped and seeded
  (enough to make 3 cups of tomatoes), or
  one 28-ounce can tomatoes, chopped, with
  juice
12 Calamata olives, pitted and halved
2 teaspoons capers, drained
5 garlic cloves, chopped
⅓ cup chopped fresh parsley
1 tablespoon chopped fresh basil
½ to ¾ pound fresh pasta
Chopped fresh parsley

Heat the oil in a sauté pan or skillet. Add the anchovies and whole garlic cloves. Cook until the garlic cloves brown and the anchovies fall apart. Add the red pepper flakes and cook a few seconds more. Add the tomatoes, olives, and capers. Simmer the sauce for 30 minutes. Add the chopped garlic, parsley, and basil to the sauce and simmer a bit longer.

Cook the fresh pasta in plenty of boiling salted water for 2 to 3 minutes or until *al dente*. Toss with half of the sauce until well coated. Arrange the pasta on a platter and pour the remaining sauce on top. Sprinkle the chopped parsley over all. *Serves 4.*

Petti de Pollo Ripiene

Stuffed Chicken Breasts

Spinach, mushrooms and goat cheese marry well in this slightly difficult and filling dish. If your menu is extensive, reduce the recipe by half, serving only half a stuffed breast per guest. The full portion is very large.

½ cup unsalted butter
¼ pound mushrooms, sliced
½ pound spinach, chopped
1 cup ricotta cheese
1 egg
⅛ teaspoon ground nutmeg
6 ounces goat cheese
½ teaspoon salt
⅛ teaspoon ground black pepper
6 whole skinned and boned chicken breasts
  (leave them whole)
½ cup dry white wine
1 cup chicken stock
1 cup heavy cream

Melt 4 tablespoons of the butter in a sauté pan or skillet. Add the mushrooms and sauté until they are lightly browned and their moisture is absorbed. Add the spinach and sauté for 1 minute more. Remove the ingredients from the pan and drain in a sieve, pressing hard with the back of a large spoon to remove the excess moisture.

In a large bowl, mix the spinach and mushroom mixture, ricotta, egg, nutmeg, goat cheese, salt, and pepper.

Pound the chicken breasts between sheets of plastic wrap or waxed paper with the side of a cleaver until they are flattened but not broken. Place one-sixth of the mixture on each breast and spread it to 1 inch from the edges. Fold the chicken in half and close with toothpicks.

Melt the remaining 4 tablespoons of butter in a sauté pan or skillet. Add the chicken. Brown on one side, then turn. When the chicken is brown on the second side, add the wine and the stock, cover, and simmer for 7 to 10 minutes, until the chicken is just done (the flesh should spring back slightly when touched).

Remove the chicken and keep it hot. Add the cream to the liquid in the pan and reduce until thick enough to coat the back of a spoon. Adjust seasoning.

Remove the toothpicks and slice the chicken crosswise in about 4 slices each. Divide among 6 plates and strain a little of the sauce over each plate. *Serves 6.*

A former Santa Fe Railroad passenger depot, designed in Spanish style, makes for some of the most interesting restaurant architecture in the Bay Area. Arches provide space for elaborate flower arrangements, and the entire setting is a showcase for the work of chef Jeremiah Tower. From his early days at Chez Panisse, Tower has figured as a founding father of the Berkeley food revolution and is now a major force on the national culinary scene. (Tower recently opened his new San Francisco restaurant, Stars.)

Innovative salads and mesquite-grilled foods are the mainstays of the menu, which is based on simple but striking combinations of ingredients. Tower's dishes are impossible to pigeonhole according to traditional categories. Featuring the freshest ingredients and beautiful presentation, the food here inspires even the most elegant patrons to reach their forks across the table and spear a taste of their companions' meal.

Compliments of

SANTA FE BAR & GRILL

BERKELEY

Warm Grilled Vegetable Salad with Grilled Goat Cheese

This is a spectacular salad when presented on a large plate. The recipe given is for one or two people; just multiply by the number of guests. Take care when grilling the vegetables; they scorch easily, especially over mesquite charcoal.

1 zucchini (as small as possible)
1 yellow or crookneck squash (as small as possible)
1 pattypan squash (as small as possible)
1 red bell pepper or pimiento
1 baby leek
2 to 3 leaves of *radicchio*
1 Japanese eggplant (as small as possible)
Olive oil
Salt and pepper
Chopped fresh thyme
One ½-inch-thick round of goat cheese

Vinaigrette

½ cup olive oil
2 tablespoons fresh lemon juice
Salt and pepper

Light a mesquite charcoal fire in an open grill. Cut all the vegetables except the radicchio in halves or quarters, depending on their size. Blanch all the vegetables except the eggplant and radicchio in salted water for 3 minutes, or until half cooked. Remove and drain in a colander. Blanch the radicchio for 1 minute; drain.

Place the eggplant in an ovenproof dish. Brush the eggplant lightly with olive oil and sprinkle with salt, pepper, and thyme. Bake in a preheated 350° oven for 15 minutes, or until almost tender.

Sprinkle the goat cheese with pepper, thyme, and olive oil. Wrap in the blanched radicchio leaves. Brush the remaining blanched vegetables lightly with olive oil, then sprinkle with salt, pepper, and thyme. Mix together the ingredients for the vinaigrette.

Grill the goat cheese packet until the cheese is soft, 1 minute or less. Grill all the vegetables until they are just tender and browned with grill marks. Remove them from the grill and toss them gently in the vinaigrette. Arrange the goat cheese in the center of a plate and surround with the vegetables. Serve immediately. *Serves 2 as a first course.*

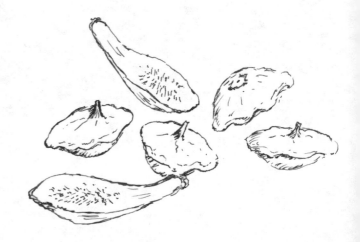

Duck Breast and Peppered Mango Salad

Another gorgeous salad. Fresh, dressed greens are surrounded by overlapping slices of mango and topped with thin slices of rare duck breast.

Mango Marinade

Salt and ground black pepper
¼ teaspoon ground cloves
½ teaspoon dry mustard
Juice of 2 limes
1 minced *serrano* or *jalapeño* chili, or to taste

2 mangos, peeled and thinly sliced
2 whole duck breasts, bone in
Peanut oil for sautéing
¾ cup hazelnut or walnut oil
3 tablespoons fresh lemon juice
Salt and freshly ground pepper to taste
4 handfuls greens (watercress, *mâche*, dandelion)

Mix all the ingredients for the marinade together and marinate the mango slices for 2 to 3 hours.

Roast the duck breasts for 10 minutes in a preheated 450° oven. Remove and cool, and then bone the breasts.

Just before serving, sauté the duck breast halves skin-side down in a small amount of oil for 3 to 5 minutes, or until the skin is crisp and most of the fat is rendered. Mix together the hazelnut oil, lemon juice, and salt and pepper and dress the greens. Place the greens on 4 serving plates and arrange the slices of mango on the greens. Thinly slice the duck and arrange the slices on the greens.
Serves 4 as a first course.

Chicken Paillards with Ancho Chili Butter

Various garnishes are suitable with chicken paillards, but at the Santa Fe they are usually served with grilled vegetables or French fries.

When grilling, remove excess marinade to avoid a flare-up from the hot coals. If a flare-up occurs and you are using a kettle-type grill with a cover, put the cover on and close the top vents for a few seconds. If using a hibachi-type grill, spray the coals with a plant mister.

3 large whole chicken breasts, skinned, boned, and halved (6 pieces)

Marinade for Chicken

¼ cup olive oil
1 tablespoon *ancho* chili powder (available in Latino groceries)

Chili-Butter Sauce

1 to 2 tablespoons *ancho* chili powder
¾ cup (1½ sticks) unsalted butter
Salt

Marinade for Vegetables

½ cup olive oil
1 tablespoon chopped fresh herbs (basil, tarragon, rosemary, etc.)

Selected vegetables for grilling: fennel, red bell peppers, summer squashes, eggplant, mushrooms
Lemon or lime wedges

Put the chicken pieces between 2 pieces of heavy plastic or paper and pound with the side of a cleaver to a thickness of about ⅜ inch.

To prepare the chicken marinade, mix the olive oil and chili powder in a pan just large enough to hold the paillards in one layer. Marinate the chicken for 3 hours in the refrigerator, turning several times.

Make the chili-butter sauce by combining the chili powder and the butter with salt to taste and leaving it to sit for a couple of hours. It should be soft to serve.

Prepare the vegetable marinade by combining the olive oil and herbs. Parboil the vegetables for 3 minutes, drain in a colander, and place in the vegetable marinade for about 2 hours.

Thirty minutes before cooking, light a mesquite charcoal fire in an open grill and remove the chicken from the refrigerator. Drain the vegetables well in a colander and cook them on the grill, spacing their timing according to the time it takes them to cook. When the vegetables are done, put the paillards on the grill and cook for 1 to 2 minutes on each side. Cooking time will vary according to the thickness of the chicken.

Put the chicken on hot plates, with the vegetables surrounding, and spoon chili-butter sauce on each serving of chicken. Garnish with lemon or lime wedges. *Serves 6.*

This is where many Berkeley chefs come to eat after work. The next day, you may find their menus reflecting what they have eaten here. This well-respected restaurant occupies a former bar called "Harry's Pearl of the Orient." The vinyl booths, gas fireplace, and dance floor remain, but the past ends there. Stunning Thai dishes balancing hot, sour, and salty flavors with accents of the exotic (lemon grass, galangal, coconut milk) send diners diving for their Thai beers, mopping their brows, and ordering seconds. Almost unassisted, this restaurant sparked a local cult of chili lovers. Not all the dishes are incendiary, however, and some feature fascinating complexities of flavor without chilies.

Compliments of

SIAM CUISINE
BERKELEY

Tom Kar Gai

Thai Chicken Soup

This sublimely simple chicken soup, rich with coconut milk and piquant with lime, would be an exotic beginning for any meal, or it could be the star of a simple meal. Much of its charm comes from cooking the chicken accurately. It should be just done. Do not cook the soup beyond the point at which it comes to a boil. Those who like chili will enjoy a sprinkling of red pepper flakes.

1½ cups unsweetened coconut milk
2 cups chicken broth
2 tablespoons fresh *galangal*, chopped, then puréed in a blender
4 ounces boneless chicken breast, cut in finger-sized pieces
¼ cup sliced bamboo shoots, drained
3 tablespoons fish sauce
3 tablespoons fresh lime juice
Cilantro sprigs or dried red pepper flakes

In a large saucepan, heat the coconut milk with the broth and the galangal. Do not boil. Add the chicken, bamboo shoots, fish sauce, and lime juice. Heat the mixture slowly until it just comes to a boil. Serve with a garnish of cilantro sprigs or red pepper flakes. *Serves 4.*

Salty Beef

Garnished with a sprinkle of red pepper flakes and wedges of lime, this dish is a knockout! There is an unusual technique involved here, a marinating process wherein the marinade is dried out of the beef, a trick the recipe tester enjoyed learning.

To fit this dish into an Asian menu is no problem, but a Western menu may require some insulation in the form of an intervening course of cold fish or perhaps an ice. It would also be interesting to serve some fresh tropical fruit with the beef.

Don't be put off by the "exotic" smell of the meat as it marinates in the fish sauce. The aroma dissipates upon frying. (See the Ingredients section on fish sauce.)

1 pound flank steak
1 tablespoon sugar
6 tablespoons fish sauce
2 tablespoons ground coriander
2 cups vegetable oil
Dried red pepper flakes (optional)
Lime wedges
Cilantro sprigs

Thinly slice the flank steak at an angle across the grain. Place the slices in one layer in an ovenproof pan. Mix together the sugar, fish sauce, and coriander and pour over the flank steak. Place in a preheated 175° to 200° oven and leave until the meat is dry, turning occasionally; this will take 3 to 4 hours.

When ready to serve, heat the oil in a deep, heavy pot. Fry the flank steak in the oil, turning until the meat is browned. Remove the beef, drain on paper towels to remove excess oil, and serve immediately, garnished, if desired, with red pepper flakes, lime wedges, and cilantro. *Serves 4 as an appetizer.*

Chicken Curry

Very hot, very complex, very unusual—these are the only ways to describe this delicious curry. You'll just have to try it. The hardest part is finding the ingredients—they are available in Asian markets.

6 to 7 small dried red peppers
1 teaspoon salt
1 tablespoon sliced fresh or dried lemon grass
1 teaspoon dried *galangal* (*laos* powder)
1 teaspoon dried lime peel
1 tablespoon ground coriander
3½ tablespoons chopped garlic
½ small red onion, sliced
1 teaspoon ground fennel
5½ cups unsweetened coconut milk
2 cups water
3 to 4 chicken breast halves, skinned, boned, and cut into 1-inch dice
2 tablespoons fish sauce
1 cup sliced bamboo shoots
¼ cup basil leaves
3 chopped *jalapeño* chilies
¼ cup crumbled dried lime leaves

Place the dried peppers in boiling water to cover for 1 minute, then seed and chop them. Mix with the salt, lemon grass, galangal, lime peel, coriander, garlic, red onion, and fennel. Set aside.

In a large saucepan, boil the coconut milk with the 2 cups water over low heat for 5 to 10 minutes. Set aside ½ cup. In a wok or skillet, stir-fry the chili mixture with the ½ cup coconut milk until well mixed. Add the chicken and the remaining coconut milk. Stir-fry until boiling, then add the fish sauce and bamboo shoots. Transfer to a platter and sprinkle with basil leaves, chopped chilies, and lime leaves. *Serves 3 to 4.*

Chicken with Sweet Basil

This dish is incendiary; the wine has not been created that could stand up to it. Strictly a beer-drinking proposition! Some hot-food advice: Cook plenty of rice. It quenches the fire better than beer or water. Also be warned that sautéing chili peppers, as in this recipe, produces very pungent fumes.

¼ cup vegetable oil
½ to 1 teaspoon dried red pepper flakes or to taste
2 teaspoons chopped garlic
1 pound boneless chicken, cut into ½-inch by 2-inch strips
4 to 6 *jalapeño* peppers, cut lengthwise and seeded
3 tablespoons fish sauce
Leaves from 4 stems of basil

Heat the oil in a sauté pan or skillet. Add the red pepper and garlic and stir quickly so they will not burn; add the chicken immediately. Add the jalapeños and sauté until the chicken is half done, about 2 to 3 minutes (the chicken should be lightly brown, but still soft). Add the fish sauce and cook 2 more minutes. Add the basil leaves, stir twice, remove from the heat, and serve. *Serves 4.*

Compliments of

SPENGER'S
FISH GROTTO
BERKELEY

❧

You can't discuss Berkeley restaurants without including Spenger's. Big, noisy, and boisterous, Spenger's retains that after-the-Big-Game atmosphere year round. It is enormously popular, and dinner parties are often made up in order to take advantage of the reservation policy, which requires a minimum of six diners. Otherwise, waits up to an hour are not uncommon, and Spenger's has a huge bar area to accommodate waiting patrons until a table is available. Once you are seated, service is efficient, portions are ample and reasonably priced, and the supply of sourdough bread is endless. No desserts are offered at Spenger's, but no one has ever left hungry!

Cold Poached Salmon with Cucumber– Sour Cream Sauce

A simple, basic recipe for a standby of buffet entertaining. Its quality depends on the quality of the salmon used.

6 salmon fillets, 5 to 8 ounces each, or one
   3-pound section or whole fish
Juice of 1 lemon
4 to 6 bay leaves
Pinch of salt

Cucumber–Sour Cream Sauce

1 large cucumber, peeled, seeded, and
   chopped
2 cups sour cream, at room temperature
½ onion, chopped
Pinch of salt

Place the salmon in a large deep pan and cover with cold water. Add the lemon juice, bay leaves, and salt. Bring to a boil, lower heat, and poach for about 10 minutes depending on the thickness of the fish—a small whole salmon should cook for about 20 minutes. The fish should be a bit translucent in the center when done. Carefully remove the fish with a slotted spatula and let it cool.

Mix together all the ingredients for the sauce and serve it with the salmon. *Serves 6.*

Compliments of

WALKER'S PIE SHOP
ALBANY

Walker's is a timeless touch of Americana. This neighborhood institution serves unassuming, moderately priced meals to its loyal customers. Take-out cream pies and berry pies are a mainstay. Dinner at eight may be the fashion elsewhere in town, but that is the hour when this home-style restaurant begins to lock up for the night. Tastes and politics are debated endlessly in Berkeley, but no one here would challenge the staying power of Walker's.

Rhubarb Pie

Rhubarb's acidity and astringency make it a good choice to end a heavy menu, and rhubarb pie is a natural for vanilla ice cream.

1 recipe Pie Dough, page 80
1 cup sugar
¼ teaspoon ground nutmeg
½ teaspoon salt
1 tablespoon cornstarch
1 tablespoon tapioca
¼ cup water, if using fresh rhubarb
4 cups rhubarb, fresh or thawed frozen
1 tablespoon butter

Prepare the pie dough. Use 1 circle of dough to line a 10-inch pie pan. Roll the second dough ball to use as the top crust. Mix the sugar, nutmeg, salt, cornstarch, and tapioca together in a bowl, adding the ¼ cup water if using fresh rhubarb. Stir this mixture into the rhubarb. Pour the rhubarb into the pie shell. Dot with butter and cover with the top crust, crimping the edges of the two crusts together. Slash the top or cut a center hole to vent the steam while cooking. Bake for 45 to 55 minutes in a preheated 375° oven, until the top crust is golden brown. *Makes 6 to 8 servings.*

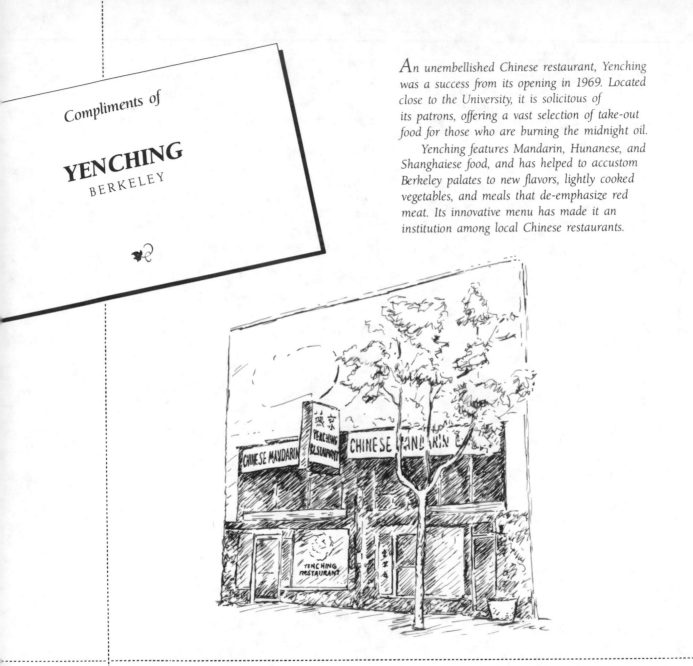

Compliments of

YENCHING

BERKELEY

An unembellished Chinese restaurant, Yenching was a success from its opening in 1969. Located close to the University, it is solicitous of its patrons, offering a vast selection of take-out food for those who are burning the midnight oil.

Yenching features Mandarin, Hunanese, and Shanghaiese food, and has helped to accustom Berkeley palates to new flavors, lightly cooked vegetables, and meals that de-emphasize red meat. Its innovative menu has made it an institution among local Chinese restaurants.

Minced "Squab" Appetizer

An imitation of squab that is actually reminiscent of the real thing, and great fun to eat. The hardest part of the recipe is cutting everything to the right size.

4 ounces dried black mushrooms
½ cup canned water chestnuts, drained
½ cup sliced bamboo shoots, drained
8 ounces boneless chicken breast
5¼ cups vegetable oil
2 teaspoons soy sauce
2 teaspoons rice wine or dry sherry
1 teaspoon Oriental sesame oil
½ teaspoon chopped garlic
½ teaspoon chopped fresh ginger
1 green onion, chopped
1-ounce package bean threads
12 red leaf lettuce leaves

Soak the mushrooms in warm water to cover until softened, about 30 minutes. Drain; save the liquid for another use. Mince the mushrooms, water chestnuts, and bamboo shoots. Chop the chicken breast into pieces the size of rice kernels. Preheat a medium-sized wok with ¼ cup of the vegetable oil.

In a medium-sized bowl, mix the minced mushrooms, water chestnuts, bamboo shoots, and chicken with the soy sauce, rice wine, and sesame oil.

Sauté the garlic, ginger, and green onion in the wok for 1 minute. Add the chicken mixture to the wok. Sauté, stirring vigorously, until there is no pinkness in the chicken.

In a deep, heavy pot, heat the remaining 5 cups of vegetable oil until almost smoking. Deep-fry the bean threads; they will puff up and double in size immediately. Remove from the pot with a slotted spoon and drain them on paper towels.

Place the fried bean threads on a platter and spoon the chicken mixture on top. Place the red leaf lettuce leaves on a second platter. To serve, place 1 tablespoon cooked chicken mixture and bean threads onto 1 lettuce leaf, roll up, and eat pancake style. *Serves 2.*

Mandarin Green Beans, Szechwan Style

Aside from the trouble of deep-frying, this is an easy dish to execute—and easier to eat! It might be worthwhile to try steaming the beans rather than frying them. The bean paste sauce is available in Chinese markets.

2 pounds Blue Lake green beans or Chinese long beans
5 cups vegetable oil
1 small piece fresh ginger, chopped
2 green onions, chopped
1 tablespoon hot bean-paste sauce
1 tablespoon sugar
½ tablespoon salt
1 tablespoon dry sherry
2 tablespoons soy sauce
1 tablespoon Oriental sesame oil
½ cup water

Cut the green beans on the diagonal into 3- to 4-inch lengths. In a deep, heavy pot, heat the vegetable oil until almost smoking. Deep-fry the beans in the hot oil for 4 minutes, remove with a slotted spoon, and drain on paper towels.

In a small bowl mix the ginger, green onions, hot bean paste, sugar, salt, sherry, soy sauce, and sesame oil together. Place the beans, water, and bean paste mixture into a sauté pan or skillet. Cook and stir for 3 minutes over high heat and serve. *Serves 6 to 8.*

Traveling together in Europe for two years as fashion models, Zachary Zachowski and Barbara Gabel pursued an unlikely diversion in their spare time: perfecting the recipe for Chicago-style stuffed pizza. When they finally returned to the United States, they decided their product was ready for the public market, and they opened a restaurant to showcase it. Even native Chicagoans praise the menu here. The success of the first pizzeria has led to a second one at the other end of town, just across the Berkeley city limits. Further proof that eclectic influences can be extended to all cuisines: Zachary's stuffed spinach pizza with pesto sauce.

Compliments of

ZACHARY'S CHICAGO PIZZA

BERKELEY

OAKLAND

Stuffed Pizza

Here is a unique pizza, a sort of Chicago-style calzone. The tricky part is making sure the top crust, which cooks under a layer of tomato sauce, is cooked through. We determined in testing that rolling the top crust thinner than the bottom is helpful. We also recommend filling the pizza with something more than just cheese, as it helps to fill the pan and gives the crust some support, not to mention making a more interesting pizza.

Crust

1 tablespoon sugar
1 package (1 tablespoon) active dry yeast
2 cups lukewarm water (105° to 115°)
¼ cup vegetable oil
4 to 6 cups unbleached all-purpose flour

Tomato Sauce

2 tablespoons olive oil
1 garlic clove, minced
One 28-ounce can crushed tomatoes and
    added purée
1½ teaspoons minced fresh oregano
1½ teaspoons minced fresh basil
¼ teaspoon freshly ground black pepper

2½ cups shredded whole-milk mozzarella
    cheese
¼ cup freshly grated Parmesan cheese
¼ cup freshly greated Romano cheese
Spinach Pesto Sauce, following (optional)

To make the crust, dissolve the sugar and yeast in the water in a large bowl; let stand until bubbly. Stir in the oil. Stir in 4 cups of the flour until smooth. Stir in the remaining flour as needed to form a stiff dough. Knead on a lightly floured surface until smooth and elastic. Put into a greased bowl. Turn the dough once to coat the top with oil and allow to rise until doubled in size.

To make the tomato sauce, heat the olive oil in a large saucepan and sauté the garlic lightly. Stir in the tomatoes, oregano, basil, salt, and pepper. Simmer for 30 minutes or until very thick.

Punch down the dough and let it rest for 10 minutes. On a lightly floured surface, roll two-thirds of the dough into a 16-inch circle. Fit this into a 12- to 14-inch deep-dish pizza pan. Make sure that the dough is pressed against the sides of the pan and that it extends over the rim.

Mix the cheeses and spread evenly over the dough. Roll the remaining dough on a lightly floured surface to form a 14-inch circle. Place over the filled dough. Seal the edges of the dough together and cut off any excess dough near the top rim of the pan.

Pour the tomato sauce over the top layer of dough and, if desired, top with spinach pesto sauce. Bake in a preheated 450° oven for 25 to 30 minutes, or until the crust is golden. *Serves 6.*

Spinach Pesto Sauce

¼ cup pine nuts
2 to 3 garlic cloves, chopped
¾ cup olive oil
1 cup chopped spinach
¾ cups basil leaves
¼ cup freshly grated Parmesan cheese
¼ cup freshly grated Romano cheese
Salt and pepper

Grind the pine nuts, garlic, and olive oil in a blender or food procesor until smooth. Add the spinach and basil and purée until smooth. Then add the cheeses, finishing the mixing by hand if the pesto is too thick for the machine to handle. Add salt and pepper to taste. *Makes about 2 cups, enough for 2 large pizzas.*

NOTE: This sauce may be frozen, but it is best to freeze without the cheeses added.

Lois Marcus, Paul T. Johnston, and Ruth Dorman

RESTAURANT INDEX

A LA CARTE
1453 Dwight Way
Berkeley
548-2322

AUGUSTA'S
2955 Telegraph Avenue
Berkeley
548-3140

BAY WOLF RESTAURANT
3853 Piedmont
Oakland
655-6004

BETTE'S OCEANVIEW DINER
1807A Fourth Street
Berkeley
644-3230

BREAD GARDEN
2912 Domingo Avenue
Berkeley
548-3122

BRITT-MARIE'S
1369 Solano Avenue
Albany
527-1314

BROADWAY TERRACE CAFE
5891 Broadway Terrace
Oakland
652-4442

CHEESE BOARD
1504 Shattuck Avenue
Berkeley
549-3183

CHEZ PANISSE
1517 Shattuck Avenue
Berkeley
548-5525

CHIN SZCHAWN
1166 Solano Avenue
Albany
525-0909

CHRISTOPHER'S CAFE
1843 Solano Avenue
Berkeley
526-9444

COCOLAT
1481 Shattuck Avenue
Berkeley
843-3265

CURDS AND WHEY
6311 College Avenue
Oakland
652-6311

FATAPPLE'S
1346 Martin Luther King Jr. Way
Berkeley
526-2260

FOURTH STREET GRILL
1820 Fourth Street
Berkeley
849-0526

GERTIE'S CHESAPEAKE BAY CAFE
1919 Addison Street
Berkeley
841-2722

GIOVANNI'S
2420 Shattuck Avenue
Berkeley
843-6678

HUNAN PALACE
1556 Solano Avenue
Albany
525-2330

INN KENSINGTON
293 Arlington Avenue
Kensington
527-5919

JAVA
843 San Pablo Avenue
Albany
525-8557

MESA
3909 Grand Avenue
Oakland
652-5223

METROPOLE
2271 Shattuck Avenue
Berkeley
848-3080

NADINE RESTAURANT
2400 San Pablo Avenue
Berkeley
549-2807

NAKAPAN
1921 Martin Luther King Jr. Way
Berkeley
548-3050

NARSAI'S
385 Colusa Avenue
Kensington
527-7900

NEW ORLEANS BAR AND GRILL
2088 Mountain Boulevard
Oakland
339-9151

NORMAN'S
College and Alcatraz avenues
Berkeley
655-5291

OMNIVORE
3015 Shattuck Avenue
Berkeley
848-4346

PASTA SHOP
5940 College Avenue
Oakland
547-4005

PICANTE TAQUERIA & CANTINA
1328 Sixth Street
Berkeley
526-9779

POULET
1685 Shattuck Avenue
Berkeley
845-5932

RAMONA'S
1329 Gilman Avenue
Berkeley
524-7732

RIERA'S
1539 Solano Avenue
Berkeley
527-1467

RISTORANTE VENEZIA
1902 University Avenue
Berkeley
644-3093

CAFFE VENEZIA
1903 University Avenue
Berkeley
849-4681

SANTA FE BAR & GRILL
1310 University Avenue
Berkeley
841-4740

SIAM CUISINE
1181 University Avenue
Berkeley
548-3278

SPENGER'S FISH GROTTO
1919 Fourth Street
Berkeley
845-7771

WALKER'S PIE SHOP
1491 Solano Avenue
Albany
525-4647

YENCHING
2017 Shattuck Avenue
Berkeley
848-2200

ZACHARY'S CHICAGO PIZZA
5801 College Avenue
Oakland
655-6385

COOKBOOKS FROM ARIS BOOKS/HARRIS PUBLISHING

The Book of Garlic by Lloyd J. Harris. A compilation of recipes, lore, history, medicinal concoctions, and much more. *"Admirably researched and well written."*—Craig Claiborne in *The New York Times*. 286 pages, paper $9.95.

The International Squid Cookbook by Isaac Cronin. A charming collection of recipes and culinary information. 96 pages, paper $7.95.

Mythology and Meatballs: A Greek Island Diary/Cookbook by Daniel Spoerri. A marvelous, magical travel/gastronomic diary with fascinating recipes, anecdotes, and mythologies. 238 pages, cloth $16.95, paper $10.95.

The California Seafood Cookbook by Isaac Cronin, Jay Harlow, and Paul Johnson. The definitive recipe and reference guide to fish and shellfish of the Pacific. 288 pages, cloth $20.00, paper $12.95.

The Feast of the Olive by Maggie Blyth Klein. A complete recipe and reference guide to using fine olive oils and a variety of cured olives. 223 pages, cloth $16.95, paper $10.95.

The Art of Filo Cookbook by Marti Sousanis. International entrées, appetizers, and desserts wrapped in flaky pastry. 144 pages, paper $9.95.

Chèvre! The Goat Cheese Cookbook by Laurel Chenel and Linda Siegfried. A marvelous collection of international recipes using goat cheese. 119 pages, paper $9.95.

Ginger East to West by Bruce Cost. A complete, fascinating reference guide to ginger—its mystique, history, and important role in international cuisine. Includes over 80 marvelous recipes. 192 pages, cloth $17.95, paper $10.95.

From a Baker's Kitchen by Gail Sher. A comprehensive guide to the art of baking. 224 pages, paper $11.95.

Chef Wolfe's New American Turkey Cookery by Ken Wolfe and Olga Bier. Carefully illustrated techniques, delicious recipes, and basic culinary sense bring our all-American bird into the 21st century. 156 pages, paper $8.95.

The Grilling Book by A. Cort Sinnes. A guide to the techniques, tools, and tastes of today's American grilling phenomenon. 192 pages, paper $10.95.

ARIS BOOKS　　　1621 Fifth Street, Berkeley, California